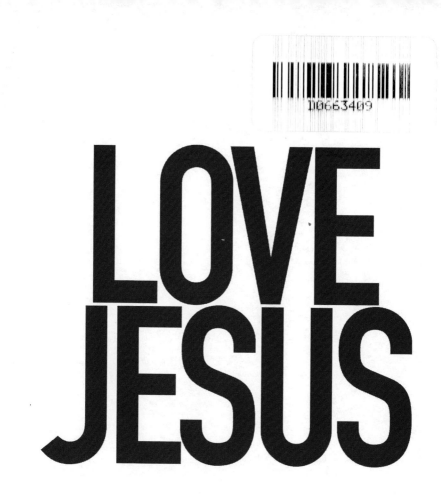

LOVE JESUS

DR. HAL HADDEN

LOVE JESUS

It is all about building relationships

FOREWORD BY DARRELL WALTRIP

What Others Are Saying
about *Love Jesus* and Dr. Hal Hadden

"The Bible says that iron sharpens iron, and that's the spirit Hal Hadden brings to *Love Jesus*. Instead of settling for the easy answers, Hal consistently challenges readers to move deeper into their relationship with Jesus. It's not always a comfortable message, but it's a message every believer can—and should—take to heart."
—*Dave Ramsey, best-selling author and nationally syndicated radio show host*

"Hal Hadden and I have had a passion to see men walk with Jesus for many years. His whole career has been about equipping men to be disciples and leaders for Christ. We even partnered in founding The National Coalition of Ministries to Men twenty years ago. I can personally vouch for Hal. He's a man of God who wants to help *all* of us to Love Jesus."
— *Patrick Morley, best-selling author of twenty books including* The Man in the Mirror, *and founder and executive chairman of* Man in the Mirror

"Day by day and year after year, Hal Hadden has invested his life in pointing men and women toward a genuine walk with Jesus. Now, Hal continues to woo and warn, encourage and enlighten all who will listen by enjoying a conversation through the pages of this book. No doubt many will discover in it help toward the kind of walk with Jesus they've always wanted."
—*Nancy Guthrie, Bible teacher and author of the* Seeing Jesus in the Old Testament Bible *study series*

"In our rapidly changing world, we can lose sight of the simple requirements of our faith. Social media, big church buildings, and fancy conferences are not the essence of what is important. Love Jesus reminds us of the simple but profound call to love Jesus and love each other."
—*Dan Miller, author and coach (48Days.com)*

"Author Hal Hadden is a person who has spent hours and hours meeting with men over a long career. With this background, he brings his life experiences and thoughts together to help his reader understand what true faith in Jesus Christ is all about and how to be a follower of Jesus who makes a difference in every arena of life. Using a nonthreatening style, he weaves together his own story, his experiences in ministry, and biblical truths to help many guys in their faith. Study questions within each section of his book will also help men/women use this book in a small group setting. I commend Hal and recommend his book."

—*Denny Rydberg, president emeritus, Young Life*

"'Is there no balm in Gilead?' 'Is there no physician there?' 'Why then is there no healing for the wound of my people?' . . . applicable questions from Jeremiah 8:22 NIV. Applicable answers to heal the wounded soul come from knowing Jesus Christ. Hal Hadden brings to light that relationship through his strengths—his teachings, his leadership. I've known Hal Hadden for many decades, known his primary aim, which is to set men free by pointing them to Christ. It's his theme. It's his banner. He cares deeply about people, evident in his readiness to reach out in friendship and to come alongside as a counselor and guide. His writings are a natural extension of the life-long commitment he has to people—not just as a learned man, but as one who has walked the path, tread the deep waters, and run the race. Through his writing, Hal Hadden is a one-to-one, heart-to-heart, spirit-to-spirit teacher, relating the truth of the saving knowledge of Jesus Christ."

—*Annette H. Valentine, author and interior designer*

"Hal Hadden's life and work demonstrate one compelled by his relationship with the Lord. When he engages others, it is from a place of genuine love. A love which exists because of the relationship he has with our Heavenly Father. His ability to engage, encourage, love, and challenge others comes out of that relationship. *Love Jesus* will take you to that relationship. Read it."

—*Kristin Cazana, national executive director, Becoming Like Christ, an equipping ministry for women*

"I have known Hal for more than forty years. I have watched him passionately give of himself to so many people in order that they might follow Jesus more closely. Hal is anything but lukewarm. He is a reminder to all of us that God will use those who are whole-heartedly pursuing him."
—*Bill Haslam, governor of Tennessee*

"Hal Hadden uses an engaging and conversational style to explore the rich dynamics of the relationship the triune God of Scripture offers to those who have come to know him. As followers of Jesus, we are privileged to enjoy intimacy with the Father, the Son, and the Holy Spirit, and Hal guides and encourages his readers to develop this intimacy in very practical and biblical ways. The group discussion questions at the end of each chapter make these concepts applicable and transferable."
—*Dr. Kenneth Boa, Reflections Ministries, Atlanta*

"Hal Hadden's life is a testament to the idea that loving relationships change lives. In *Love Jesus*, he speaks from the overflow of his heart and offers us this simple yet powerful reminder—authentic life is found in the most loving of all relationships—a relationship with Jesus. In the pages of *Love Jesus* you will find stirring word pictures that emphasize the eternal truth that Jesus loves you and always will! So grab a cup of coffee (Hal would approve!), find a comfortable chair, and make an investment in a relationship that lasts."
—*Dr. Craig Fry, president of Christian Leadership Concepts (CLC)*

"There are people who talk about knowing Jesus, and there are people who know Jesus. There are people who talk about helping others know Jesus, and there are people who help others know Jesus. In almost twenty years of ministry, I can't think of many people who know Jesus and help others know Jesus like my friend Hal Hadden does. Hal is a man of God who, far from seeing himself as an expert, continues to learn. But it is his humble, learning posture that actually does make him an expert in the things about which he writes in this book. A church elder, a faithful husband and father, a friend to many, a lover of Jesus, and a lifetime evangelist and discipler and leader of men—Hal's passion remains to know Jesus and to help others know Jesus. If that is your desire also, I recommend this book, which reflects a lifetime of faithfulness and service, wholeheartedly to you. I pray that in its reading, you, too, will come to know Jesus and help others know him."

—*Scott Sauls*, *senior pastor of Christ Presbyterian Church in Nashville, Tennessee, and author of* Jesus Outside the Lines

Relational Publishers
P.O. Box 582
Brentwood, Tennessee 37024

Bible verses cited in this book are from the New International Version (NIV)

Cover design by Thomas Ryan
Inside graphic illustrations by Bill Collier
Page layout by Mike Towle

Printed in the United States of America

*To the main women in my life: Linda, my wife;
and Christy, Lana, and Libby—my three daughters*

To the men in Christian Leadership Concepts (CLC)

To the women in Becoming Like Christ (BLC)

*To the men at the Franklin Fellowship
meeting at Darrell Waltrip's house*

Contents

Foreword

HAL HADDEN IS A TRUE MAN'S MAN. NOT ONLY THAT, HE'S A MAN
OF God who loves people and has a heart for their faith
walk. Hal has been coming to my house once a week for
more than thirty years to teach sixty-plus men about how to have a
relationship with Jesus Christ and how to grow in that relationship.

Hal's teachings are straight out of the Bible, and his style is to
make guys feel comfortable when discussing sensitive issues we all
struggle with. I know he also has the same knack for teaching and
leading discussions in other settings, with men and women alike.

When we originally started the home group at my house back
in the 1980s, we called it the "Franklin fellowship." Franklin is where
I live, about twenty miles south of Nashville. In those early days of
our fellowship studies, Hal taught on business and the marketplace.
Many of the men there were businessmen, eager to learn about connecting Sunday to Monday and how to reconcile workplace and financial challenges with the Word of God.

After teaching this for about twenty weeks, Hal saw how much
men needed to hear what God had to say about the marketplace, so
he decided to teach the book of Proverbs and apply it to the marketplace. He ended up teaching the whole book of Proverbs over a

period of more than ten years.

No one was better at teaching these biblical principles to those men than Hal. I saw it firsthand countless times. For one thing, he had walked in their shoes. He had a hand in not only leading some of those men to the Lord, but he showed others how to enhance their Jesus walk.

It was fun to see Hal and the fellowship co-leader, Leonard Isaacs, work together. Even with two strong personalities, they never disagreed on how to run things. How did they manage to do that? It was not about them and not about who was in control or who got the credit. It was about Jesus. They were there to serve him.

One year we loaded up the guys into two buses and went to Atlanta to watch a NASCAR race. That was a great time, and it had an impact on everyone there. It was men standing together and enjoying good, fun fellowship. Opportunities like that come right out of Hal's DNA.

Hal wasn't just about the meetings, though. He was about relationships and getting involved in my world. He came to many of my races, and while there he attended the chapel service for the drivers. We had lunch many times, and for years we shared a Christmas dinner and celebration together with a small group of couples.

Another thing about Hal: he is serious, but he likes to have a good time. He can handle a set of wheels, too. I like that he drives a sports car convertible and that he dresses in style.

In this home group setting, Hal has always been able to accept men no matter where they come from. As he often says, "The meeting is for those from boots to suits, no dues, no membership." Two or three thousand men have come to my house for these weekly meetings over the years. Without regard to skin color or faith background, Hal welcomes the rich, the poor, the young, the elderly, the unemployed, CEOs, painters, those with clout and those without, on and on. As one man said recently, Hal is nonjudgmental.

Here's what I really love about Hal. He is always available to help someone in need, and he is sincere about this. Over the years God has used him to just stand with men as they faced bankruptcy, divorce, job loss, death, or career change, and he's there to help one of them at any given time to begin a personal walk with Jesus.

Without question the main emphasis at the weekly meeting has been Jesus, with the Scriptures comprising Hal's only foundation for lesson plans. *Love Jesus* encapsulates all of the key biblical principles that Hal has been teaching and leading discussions on. If there's any way to take those thirty years of Hal-led ministry and boil them down into a book, this is it. *Love Jesus* will light a path for readers in the same way his ministry has shown the way for thousands of those who have come to embrace our Lord.

Hal Hadden cares about Jesus, and he is a friend to me. I am blessed to call Hal my friend and faith mentor.

—*Darrell Waltrip, American motorsports TV analyst and commentator, winner of 84 career NASCAR Cup Series races, and three-time NASCAR Cup Series champion (1981, 1982, and 1985)*

Acknowledgments

WRITING A BOOK IS A CHALLENGE FROM MANY ASPECTS. I HAD lots of help. Friends came along beside me to spur me on. Barbie Doyle, wife of my co-worker Ron Doyle, began praying for me as I began formulating the vision for the book.

When I was discouraged and had lost my way, Norene Yowell read the manuscript and encouraged me to keep going. My sister, Annette Valentine, asked about the progress of the book about every time we were together, and she was always praying for me. Debbie French, Joe Flautt, Mike Duncan, and Lana Myers read the manuscript, making suggestions but mainly telling me how it had impacted their lives, which was very encouraging. Larry Stone gave me great counsel and wisdom concerning the process and work that would be involved. I think I would have given up without these friends being on my team.

God knew I needed lots of technical help, so he sent plenty my way. Michael Neal has been there from the beginning giving me advice, helping to bring my writing into focus. Michael has been incredible! I would not have written this book without him. He spent lots of time helping me think through what I wanted to say. Mike Towle was sent to help with the editing. He was patient, encouraging, and essential to the process. He was able to edit my writing while keeping my voice. Thomas Ryan, a longtime friend, did the design work for the cover. Bill Collier, my new friend, did the graphics. I am also grateful to Dave Altizer, Austen and Bradley Weatherly, Michael Ricks, and Macey Benton from my young adult Sunday school class that produced the promotional video.

It has been a team effort with the Holy Spirit guiding all the way. I am so thankful for all expertise, love, prayer, and counsel from many.

Introduction

PICTURE YOU AND ME SITTING AT A TABLE IN A COFFEE SHOP ENJOYING good conversation over a cup of joe. We're just shooting the breeze—no agenda, just lots of freedom to be who we are, saying what we want, expressing our feelings, and listening to one another with open minds.

This has been my modus operandi for my many years of standing with men—just being friends. Rough estimate, I have probably had more than six thousand such get-togethers with thousands of people, some of them several times each. It's always in an environment of mutual exchange in which I learn as much from them as they might glean from what I have to offer about life and through the Word of God and my own relationship with Jesus Christ. I don't use the word "relationship" here lightly: A true, invested relationship with Jesus is the crux of what I will discuss here, but it is about caring about people. In that sense I hope this book will play a profound part in touching your life in a significant manner.

For many years, my heart has been to build men up to be strong men and capable leaders, but I see very few strong followers of Jesus these days. I see a lot of activity but no relationship. As I personally began to passionately pursue a love relationship with Jesus, my heart and life began to change. I then wanted others to experience what God had revealed to me and what I was experiencing. I have the same passion to see women built up in a similar manner, ably fulfilling their role as prescribed by Jesus in the New Testament.

I don't have all the answers, and I have made my fair share of boneheaded mistakes along the way. My walk with Jesus has been one of imperfection on my part, but it has been a continually perfect source of blessings and joy. In *Love Jesus* I make myself vulnerable by expressing my thoughts and exposing to you some of my insides. Not all of what I reveal about myself is what you would expect to hear from a Jesus follower who has been building up men for decades. I have my flaws and will unveil some of those to you. I do this not to seek pity or to solicit empathy via false humility, but to let you know that God is a forgiving God, and my life is an ongoing testimony to that.

My aim here, also, is to throw some questions at you that will push you out of your comfort zone. I want to encourage you to abandon your normal way of thinking and to take full account of *where* you are in life as well as *who* you are. If you were looking for a fun, nonconfrontational book with which to curl up on the couch, this isn't it. If that's what you want, though, be my guest: stop here and go grab for yourself a good novel, because it would be far easier—in terms of self-examination—to plow through than some of what I have to say in these pages. Your choice.

OK, it looks like you're sticking with me, because you are still reading this. Good for you!

You will notice that I strike a conversational tone throughout this book. At times I speak in first person when relating some of my own experiences and thoughts about a genuine walk with Jesus Christ; at other times I speak directly to you, not to patronize you but to draw you in to something dear to my heart that will hopefully touch yours as well.

The Almighty God desires a personal relationship with you. Yes, *you*! I don't even have to know you or see you face to face to have full confidence in saying to you that God wants a relationship with you—a two-way relationship, naturally! To most "Christians," God will say,

"I never knew you." That *should* scare you. Lukewarm won't cut it. Just as Jesus walked and lived with his disciples, he wants to share life with mankind—to the fullest. This intimate spiritual relationship will radically change and empower you as well as it could any other person. Fellow believers in Jesus can experience a fellowship and friendship with one another that will go beyond their comprehension; others will be drawn to what and who they see in the true believer.

Picture a big, beautiful oak tree next to a stream, with branches, leaves, and fruit attached to a healthy, sturdy trunk. Of course you can't see the roots, which are underground, but they are there and probably have more strength to them than the limbs you see above ground. The roots are the foundation of the tree. Metaphorically, let the roots be the biblical theology that helps to explain the whole picture of what God wants to say to you in revealing his mind. Theologians long have attempted to explain essential concepts in a systematic way so that we all can soak up what Scripture reveals on particular topics such as end times, salvation, and sanctification. Those subjects get covered so much, though, that they border on cliché—stuff we've heard about so many times that hearing about them again no longer provides the sizzle, which is a shame. Well, this book isn't directly about these important topics, even though scriptural verses are sprinkled here and there throughout this book, although not in such a large quantity as to suffocate readers.

Let the branches and leaves/fruit of that tree represent the actions we take in order to be obedient in applying the truth of Scripture. Be aware: this book isn't about the practices of Christianity or the application of it, even though there is application all the way through the book. This book's primary emphasis is on the all-important aspect of being a follower of Jesus and forging a genuine personal relationship with him. Can the trunk of the tree represent this relationship? Absolutely. Our relationship with Jesus is based on the foundational theological roots; a deep relationship with Jesus leads to great application. Let's fall deeper in love with Jesus and passionately pursue Him with all our heart, and let's be proactive about it. Let's not just read about it while in cruise control and then forget about it two days later.

In today's world of what I call "religious correctness," which is a close relative to political correctness, I see Christian discipleship being watered down in churches as well as outside the church walls. Discipleship has been redefined from what I think Jesus was trying to do, and I want to address that need. The most important aspect of discipleship is being in relationship with Jesus; all else flows out of that relationship. I encourage you to immerse yourself in your Jesus relationship as a 24/7 commitment—not that I expect you to be praying, reading/studying Scripture, and/or proselytizing to others every waking moment. I'm simply talking about selling yourself out to Jesus and being a BFF (best friend forever) to him, starting right now. I believe if I'm successful in lighting this spark inside of you, you will see a Jesus relationship in an entirely new light, maybe as a vivid, ongoing reality for you. Chances are, too, you will suddenly see what's being preached or taught at your current church in a new way, as you test what's being fed you from a whole new perspective. For many of you, this will involve a real-time paradigm shift.

My hope is that all eleven chapters in this book will be very positive and motivational, drawing you to a walk with Jesus that *sticks* and goes far beyond a passing fancy. Roughly the first three-quarters of the book reveals and reinforces all that goes into enhancing your personal relationship with Jesus. The last 20 percent of the book will address your friendship with others, especially in a group setting. This will give you the foundational tools (via your relationship with Jesus Christ) to share, when appropriate, your life with others by telling them what you have learned and how they, too, can come into a more personalized bond with Jesus and love him. Again, you will be challenged; if you dig deep into this, you will be chosen to bring the good news to others.

If you apply yourself to the tenets brought forth in *Love Jesus*, you should realize the following:

- Be challenged to rethink and evaluate your personal relationship with God from the biblical evidence presented;

- Be motivated to encounter Jesus in a more personal and in-depth manner;

- Realize that Jesus wants to be "with YOU";
- Realize that Jesus will be "in YOU."
- Understand the intimate relationship with God that addresses the essential family dimensions as your Father, Friend, Husband, and Brother;
- Experience a relationship with God, which includes being empowered by his Spirit to live dynamically and powerfully;
- See a vision for being in relationship with a small group of believers who pursue God and each other together, so that the relationship with God matures and overflows into authentic relationships with one another, resulting in a growing walk with God;
- Have a passion to share life with those in your circle of influence and build "as you go" relationships that will open the door for eternal purposes.

Millennials and baby boomers are rejecting the wrong Jesus because they don't see the real Jesus lived out in professing Christians. Most churches have become ineffective in communicating the truth. The church experience has become an event for a few hours a week where there is little connection with God or others.

Love Jesus casts a biblical view of God taking the initiative to come to earth to be among us, and be "with us," and then to be "in us" as we are "in him," so that we as believers can enjoy the family relationship with God that he offers as our Father, Brother, Friend, and Husband. As a follower of Jesus, you will be empowered to exchange your weak life for one in which God is working in you to be and to do what he has set forth in Scripture.

Still interested? I hope so. That said, let's get started. And, by the way, thanks for joining me for some coffee. Now it's time to get fed with God's Word, allowing it to guide you toward a never-ending embrace of Jesus Christ . . . for real.

Part I

A Real and Unreal Relationship with God

1

The Creator Desires a Relationship with You

"One thing I know. I was blind but now I see."
— The blind man
JOHN 9:25

❦

I T IS ONE THING TO FAIL; IT'S TOTALLY ANOTHER THING TO BE SHAMED! Failure says, "I messed up" or "I couldn't do something." Shame says, "I am no good. I am a loser. I am not worth much."

"Loser" was my identity growing up and a significant part of my adult life. Everything I did revolved around me as a loser trying to avoid failure so that I wouldn't be shamed any more. Success was not my motivation. Chances are that at some level you can identify with my journey because most of us have, at one time or another, sensed shame from a failure such as adultery, bankruptcy, divorce, or some sort of sexual involvement issue.

I was in grade school when I first realized there was something wrong with me. The teacher would have the students read out loud; when it was my turn, I would read a lot slower than the others. I had to: reading was very difficult for me, even when reading silently to myself. I couldn't properly pronounce many of the words, and sometimes I stuttered. A few of my classmates would look at me and laugh, and I would turn all red. I hated reading out loud and would do anything I could to get out of it. That included telling the teacher I couldn't read because I didn't have my glasses, when in fact I didn't even own any. All I could think was, God doesn't have time for me because I am so messed up and too insignificant! There were long stretches of time when I believed no one valued me or wanted to hang out with me. I was alone, even with plenty of other kids around me.

As a kid growing up, I lived in the shadows of my two older brothers. I was always comparing myself to them, and each time I was coming up short. When my younger sister came along, I really got pushed into the background of my family's dynamic. I remember wondering why there were so many pictures around the house of my brothers, yet so few of me. After my sister was born, her photos started appearing all over the place as well. Did my parents get a new camera and take a photography course when my sister came along, or was she just so much more valuable than me? I felt pretty marginalized.

Why would a big, powerful God want to be in a relationship with someone like me? That was my thinking during much of my youth. When I would contemplate what was going on in my heart and in my head, I could rationalize why he wouldn't want to be involved in my life. Besides, I was pretty small and insignificant compared to him and, well, everyone else.

I really didn't think much about God, and I wasn't sure he existed. If he did exist, I thought, he didn't seem essential to my life or the lives of anyone else around me. I would think, "Is he that big and powerful? Is he knowable and personal? Maybe he is far greater and bigger than I could or can imagine."

I remember, as a twenty-year-old, two years after beginning a personal relationship with God, standing on top of Mount Princeton in Colorado at an altitude of fourteen thousand feet, wondering, "Who is this God? How big is he really, and can I be in a relationship with him?" I concluded that he is far bigger than I can imagine. He wants to know me and all of us in a far deeper way than we can imagine.

Your own story or feelings are likely different from mine, but I suspect most of us at one time or another have imagined why God wouldn't want to be in relationship with us. Maybe it's because of some sin in our lives, or perhaps we are too selfish or just don't want God in our lives. However, that doesn't stop him from pursuing you or me.

If you and I were to take a pen and draw the biggest circle possible and then put one dot in that circle indicating our understanding of God, that little dot wouldn't come close to showing how big God is relative to how small we are or how uninformed our view is of God.

In college I was a science major (chemistry, physics, and biology), and my education exposed me to some things that even today help me grasp a little more about God, or at least his creative ability, from an empirical point of view. I was convinced there was a God whenever I looked under the microscope and saw things moving or when I did a cross section of an embryo and noticed how it developed from a sperm and an egg. All of those amino acids coming together to form a human body in just the right way astounded me, yet at the same time it baffled me. When the Hubble telescope shows millions of galaxies and billions of stars, all of which he holds together (Colossians 1:16-17), I grasp that God is so much more powerful than I can imagine. It is at those times I know I have to take it by faith as to how big he is. The bottom line is this: in all God's greatness and incomprehensibility, he wants a relationship with us. He is awesomely bigger and more transcendent than we can imagine, yet so knowable and approachable.

"You want a relationship with *us*? What about a relationship with *me*?" you might ask. I did ask that. Why would the Almighty want to have a relationship with me, since I believed I was too insignificant and too ungodly for him to want to know me?

In some ways it is no big deal that I was the third son in our family, followed by a younger sister. Nevertheless, I felt insignificant and lost in the familial shuffle. I never questioned or doubted I was loved, but I felt pretty unimportant. That's because I lived in my brothers' shadows at home and at school. I wanted to be like my older brother who played football, but I found that practice didn't make perfect. I got to practice, but I didn't get to play in the games. My main role was to hold the dummy bag as blockers and runners ran my way and slammed into the heavy bag. Being tall, skinny, and slow didn't help me much in terms of playing time.

Academics weren't much help, either. Schoolwork didn't help affirm my identity, and it failed to make me think I was valued or that God might want to know me. I remember seeing a book around our house titled *Why Johnny Can't Read*. That was me: *Hal Can't Read*. When I finished high school, I was reading on a sixth-grade level. Most people get a little clout and an ego boost from some form of achievement, but I had no worthy achievements from which to draw. I sought attention by being somewhat of a "hell-raiser," which expressed itself in some destructive behavior I dished out to teachers and those different from me. Two teachers told me I would never go to college. All of this is to say, "Why would Creator-God want a relationship with me?"

I felt like the rug was pulled out from under me in my last year of high school, when my dad was transferred to Knoxville from Middle Tennessee. Moving to a new location did nothing to bolster my confidence. I felt like a loser moving away from the familiar and friends. It just so happens that during that time a former University of Tennessee basketball player and Young Life youth ministry volunteer, Charlie Scott, came to my high school to speak to and to meet students. He hung out at the smoking pit, learned my name, and made it a point to show he cared about me. He was truly a God-figure to me. Later he invited me to go to a Young Life camp in Colorado. I enthusiastically agreed because I loved adventure, travel, mountains, and girls. This place had it all, plus more.

It was at Young Life camp that I heard the gospel that says that God loves little, "insignificant" Hal. At first I couldn't comprehend that he loved me. Then I heard how he loved me so much that he gave his son to die in my place to pay not only for my hell-raising, but for my sin nature that dominated my life. Alone on the steps of an empty cabin, with tears running down my cheeks, I prayed something like this, "God, if you love me so much to die for me, I want to love you back by committing my life to you and putting my life in trust to Jesus." It was as simple as that. My life truly did a 180-degree turn on the spot: I was a new person spiritually from the inside out.

Not long after that I was accepted to the University of Tennessee. As a premed student as well as a new believer and follower of Jesus, I worked really hard. I even joined a fraternity because my brothers and friends had. After great discipline and hard work, however, my first grade report had me at a D average! So I worked harder and repeated some courses (some more than once). After two years the University of Tennessee asked me to continue my higher education at a lower institution. That might sound funny now, but it wasn't funny then. Once again, I was a loser and a failure. In my mind, I was proving right the two high school teachers who had put me down with a critical spirit, although it was true that I had given them every reason to say I didn't belong in college. Shame overwhelmed me. I was a loser!

For the next seventeen years I hid the fact that I had flunked out of UT, even though I did eventually graduate from college and seminary. I finished seminary with very good grades in my courses, but I still had a nagging sense of being a failure and a loser from my days at UT.

Notice on the front of the book that it says "Dr. Hal Hadden." I'm guessing I might be the only person in Tennessee who flunked out of UT and has a doctorate from Vanderbilt University. That is meant as humor, but as far as I know it is true. When putting a value on the two experiences at two universities, I can honestly say that on a scale of one to ten in terms of significance, with ten being the highest value, the doctorate is a one and flunking out of UT is a ten. Yes, because of my shame, seventeen years went by before I would ever tell anyone that I flunked out of UT. I kept that covered up because of shame. However, it is important for me to remember it because it truly spoke to how I viewed myself as a loser. More than that, it spoke to who God is and what he can do for a so-called "loser." Seeing God use this shameful failure is what makes it a value of ten. He knew me, loved me, and called me to himself to be one of his sons. Coming to grips with that understanding seventeen years after flunking out of college changed my whole paradigm. Being in relationship with the great Almighty God, who made me a son, is what life is all about. Being a son was my new identity. I began to live life as a son of God and not as a loser or failure or in my brothers' shadows.

I know that God, as Creator, made me and my body in a unique manner. He gave me fingerprints that no one else in the entire universe has; I even have a tailor-made voice. Now he tells me that he wants a relationship with each one of us: that is what is called a "love relationship." God choosing to send his Son to die for our sins sends a loud and clear message that he wants to be in relationship with mankind. I can pretty well understand the love relationship that my wife and I have, but to be in love with God and to know he loves me more than I can comprehend—that blows my mind. David, in Psalm 139, said it well: "You know when I sit down and when I rise; you perceive my thoughts from afar. Before a word is on my tongue you, Lord, know it completely. Such knowledge is too wonderful for me, too lofty for me to attain. How precious are your thoughts, God! How vast the sum of them! Were I to count them, they would outnumber the grains of sand." To think that God is so big, yet he made me and knows my every move, is really special. It is also a bit unnerving. Jesus's sacrificial death communicates that he loves you and me so much and wants to have a very personal, rich love relationship with us. Does he know who I am? I am just "little ole me." I was a skinny, selfish, in-the-shadows kind of guy most of my life, just one in nearly eight billion people. Why would he love me and want to share life with me?

Knowing all this—for starters, how we are created as unique among eight billion people on earth—we should be awestruck when we realize we can be in a personal, intimate relationship with God. This is flesh and blood real, not just words on this page, although it can seem the latter if we are disengaged from the truth expressed in his Word and in his actions. Yes, the Majestic One, who is transcendent and also immanent, desires to be very close and personal. The wonder of God and reality of his presence should excite us and scare us. Our sense of awe when we see who Jesus is, and when we realize the relationship we can have with him, should excite us with possibility thinking beyond our imagination.

The Creator Desires a Relationship with You

When Jesus was on the Sea of Galilee with his disciples, a furious storm appeared. At this, Jesus rebuked the winds and the waves to calm them. This powerful action by a "man" frightened the disciples and made them terrified of Jesus. They were in awe. One of them asked, "Who is this that even the wind and waves obey him?" When Thomas saw the holes in Jesus's hands, he was in wonderment and said, "My Lord and my God." When a detachment of soldiers and officials came to arrest Jesus, as depicted in John 18:6, the soldiers and others "drew back and fell to the ground" when Jesus said, "I am he." On the Mount of Transfiguration, they saw his face change and his clothes become as bright as a flash of lightning. They were awestruck! Encountering His Majesty, wonder, glory, and holiness can cause anyone to fall onto his or her knees in worship of God Almighty. Emotion, wonder, surprise, fear, and dread will come over us when we begin to understand who Jesus is. There will be an overwhelming feeling of reverence and admiration because he is so grand, so powerful. His authority, genius, and great beauty are far beyond the scope of our comprehension. To put it simply: You will know him when you see him.

The Scriptures say in a letter to the Ephesians 3:17b-18, ". . . I pray that you, being rooted and established in love, may have power, together with all the Lord's holy people, to grasp how wide and long and high and deep is the love of Christ." God as the Almighty One is in love with you and me. It *is* personal. That truth should shake us to the core. God is relational, and he wants our love in return, to love him with all our heart, mind, soul, and strength. Let that sink in for a while. In return, he loves us with a love that is so wide, long, high, and deep that we can't picture it. This awesome love relationship between the Creator and created (to include us) is the foundation of and ultimate reality for this life and the life to come. Don't miss out on it.

Group Discussion Questions:

As a group, we are individuals and a connected group. Our discussion is meant to start with an ice-beraker question, then the rational dimension of ourselves, then move to our hearts or feelings, and, lastly, to take action by stepping out and utilizing what we gained. This is only a suggestion and doesn't mean you have to start with the head or heart or feet. Most times our head and heart are the foundation for our actions.

Hook: As a group, try to describe what it would be like to sit down over dinner with the president of the United States. How would having dinner with the Creator compare to that?

1. Head. Describe what an in-depth, quality, ongoing relationship with someone to whom you are close looks like. As a group, decide on the top four characteristics of a great relationship.

2. Head. Share how grasping the fact that this Almighty, who is beyond comprehension as Creator, wants to encounter you in these four deep relational characteristics and how this will cause a paradigm shift, affecting your entire life.

3. Heart. Tell about the excitement you feel as you better understand that the Creator wants to share life with you. What feelings well up inside you?

4. Heart. It is sometimes hard to comprehend that God does want a relationship with us. This is probably due to a bad self-image or guilt or shame. Would any of you tell what you have felt or are feeling now?

5. Hand. Each of you take a minute of silent private prayer, telling God how you feel both excitement and concern about being in a relationship with him.

6. Hand. Open it up to the group to pray out loud, expressing some of what they are feeling and thinking.

2

It Is All About a Relationship with God

"My Lord and my God."
— Thomas
JOHN 20:28

T HE KEY WORD IN ALL OF SCRIPTURE AND IN ALL OF LIFE IS "relationship". Yes, that's sharing and walking through life together in a love relationship. More than likely, you have found the greatest fulfillment in life to be a good relationship with someone you care about. You are a relational being, just like our God. Through Adam and Eve, that relationship with God was broken; now it has been restored, free of charge. When you and I are in the right relationship with God, we are most fully human. In Jesus we were made to "live and move, and have our being" in God (Acts 17:28).

This relationship with God is an active love relationship that is available in any culture, any time, with anyone. It is not so fancy that the most intelligent person in the world is unable to experience it. The same goes for the most illiterate person in the world. It is a grassroots, day-in-and-day-out relationship. It is based on sound biblical theology and expressed in actions and behavior that reflect God's heart. It is not so theologically focused that the average person lacks the ability to comprehend it. It is readily discernible. It is a love relationship that involves knowing God (Jesus), following him, and fellowshipping with him. Ideas and theology contribute to our understanding of Jesus, but

9

Jesus is more than an idea. He is the one to relate to, to share life with, and to love.

Are you experiencing that deep kind of relationship with God right now? I mean 24/7, where your entire life centers around and evolves out of your relationship with God. I'll take it even a step further: Is Jesus your life; not just part of it but all of it? Does your love for him fit into the "all" category of mind, heart, soul, and strength?

Let me give you a word picture of this relationship, even knowing that few metaphors can fully describe our walk with God. I remember taking a college botany course for which part of the final exam was to identify certain trees by their Latin names. I couldn't pronounce most of them, much less identify them. Fortunately, that bad experience didn't prevent me from having a great affection for trees; I especially like the giant sequoias in Yosemite National Park (although I don't know the Latin name for them).

In this book's introduction, I described a metaphor about a tree in which the roots are the theology; the trunk is your relationship with Jesus; and the branches, leaves, and the fruit are the active responses to being in a relationship with Christ. Theology is based in Scripture. Theologians organized the truths in a systematic manner so we can better understand the full biblical teaching on a specific topic. Then we can live our lives based on God's full teaching. Without theology the relationship will God will "blow over" and not withstand conflict. Theology is essential, but knowing lots of theology is no guarantee of a relationship with God.

When I first began a love relationship with God at the Young Life Camp in Colorado, I knew very little theology. I grasped one immoveable truth, which was that God loves me as one of his sons. The proof is what Jesus did through his death and resurrection, with his Spirit confirming my position with him in my heart and my spirit. That went a long way and remains a solid foundation for me. When I doubted my salvation or my walk with him, God solidified in my mind that the moorings of my life were in him. I belonged to him and I knew I loved him. The relationship was really all I wanted and needed. I learned theology when I studied and was taught the

Word of God. The roots got deeper and healthier as I grew in my relationship with Jesus.

I am thankful for everyone who invested in me. I mentioned Charlie, my Young Life leader who reached out to me in high school. He also stuck with me in my first year of college when studies were so tough and I felt hopeless. He and other Young Life men put me on the work crew and summer staff as a lifeguard at one of the camps, where I was exposed again to the gospel and received deeper biblical teaching. These men were there for me in good times and bad. Dr. Robert Traina taught me how to study the Bible for myself. In my office I have six ten-by-ten pictures of these men and others who impacted my life. The main thing they did for me was to be a friend and point me to Jesus.

God is a Person. He is relatable and personal. True fellowship flows out of a relationship with God and believers centered on Jesus. The roots are essential but they are not the essence.

As I'm writing this, it's wintertime and I'm looking out the window. I see lots of trees without leaves or fruit. I don't see the roots, but I know they are there. I know it because the tree needs to be rooted in order to be standing; I know this because my basic knowledge of science states that trees have roots. I have faith that this tree's roots are present even though I can't see them—they are hidden underground. Likewise, the theology is true and in place whether you know it or not. It is right out of God's mind, and it is real whether we see it or not. Its existence is not contingent on our believing it into existence. The leaves and fruit are gone for now, but in season they will be back because the tree is alive and well. This is how we need to live in relationship with Jesus, and he will take care of the rest. We know that by faith; there is no other way to explain it.

A genuine relationship with God as discussed here is not about good works such as trying to look "spiritual," keeping rules, dressing demurely, having a devotional time, performing service projects, making promises to God, memorizing verses, or being the perfect helpmate. Also, it's not about how to stop smoking, quit gambling, cease stealing, or dispense with messing around. Those are for another discussion at another time. If we really know Jesus and love him while trusting him, we will obey him because it is our desire to do so. Likewise, when we fail to obey him, we still know his love continues to be unconditional. As we confess our failures, he will restore us. The fellowship with him might be hindered at any time, but the relationship always is intact.

When I think back to my story of hearing how God loved me despite his knowing my background and loved me so much that he would send his only begotten Son to die, I was humbled and overwhelmed. I could not comprehend that kind of unconditional love. In my humility and brokenness, I said to God, "I want to love you back. I want to follow the God who loves like that."

For the next six to seven years I was blown away that God loved me. The gospel was transforming my life from the inside out. What love! I had a new purpose for life: Love Jesus and honor him. It started with knowing that the manner in which I treated and approached women needed to change. They had been objects of my gratification. Also, I learned to accept that my body wasn't my own; I didn't have the freedom or desire to get drunk anymore, although I failed badly at one point, just three months after coming from the Young Life camp, at Dunbar Cave Night Club. I still remember lying on the side of the road vomiting while my friend, Bob, stood nearby with his thumb out trying to hitch a ride for us from Kentucky to Nashville.

My life was radically changed by the awareness and the experience of being in a love relationship with God, but I hadn't arrived spiritually. I would sing a hymn I learned in Young Life: "Oh, the deep, deep love of Jesus." I just couldn't get over it. He loves me. He died for me. I didn't just say it; I felt it. After a while I became accustomed to hearing about his love from Bible teachers as well as reading about it in the Bible. Through this I became confident in myself by believing that God loved me. I am a loved son of his.

I also know that God doesn't just love me; he often shows that he loves me and does hear my prayers. Mal McSwain's encouraging me to begin praying for my future wife came just three weeks after I committed my life to Jesus at Young Life's Silver Cliff Ranch on Mount Princeton in Colorado. So it was that in August seven years later I was back at the same ranch, this time as a camp counselor, when a beautiful woman, Linda, from Illinois showed up to counsel teenagers. After I returned to my hometown of Knoxville, Tennessee, Linda and I began to correspond: a year later we were married. Interestingly, I had now "met" Jesus at Silver Cliff, and then met my future wife there several years later. Prayer works.

After we married, my focus moved more to my wife and less to Jesus. To a degree, I began to think of Linda and me as becoming one; my love for Jesus was displaced by my love for her. I began to focus on loving her unconditionally. God loved me unconditionally so I could love Linda unconditionally. At the same time, I began to move away from marveling in the truth that God loved me. Over the course of the next thirty-plus years I would continue to veer away, ever so slightly, but even a slight shift multiplied by thirty-odd years can make a difference. That difference, I realized, was that I had lost my first love—that passion and awareness I had had for God. It had become too familiar and I was taking it for granted. The spark was gone. I was going through the motions much like the believers in Revelation 2, where they did many good things but had no love. Without realizing it, I had drifted backward to religious activity with no heart, much like those believers. God told those believers to remember the heights they had come from in their relationship with him, and to repent and do what they did at first (Revelation 2:4-6).

As a fifty-plus-year-old man with a strong belief in Jesus, I finally made a conscious decision to repent, to tell him I loved him, and to thank him that he loved me. I began to pour myself back into him and the Scripture. Verses began to jump out, speaking that incredible truth. I went to bed praying and thanking God for his infinite love. I told him how much I loved him. It was a rich, engaging experience. Joy overflowed in my heart. I would wake up in the morning, telling him again of my love for him in different ways and thanking him in various ways for his love for me. Was I following some prescribed process for doing this? No, I just did it. I was rejuvenated in my love for him. It was sweet, and it still is sweet.

Where are you right now in your love relationship with God? He longs for this kind of relationship with you. Did you once have it and now feel you have lost it, or at least the intensity of what you once had has died down? Have you geared down what was once an awesome love relationship to what is now simply going through the motions, such that your relationship with God has become impersonal? If any of this is so, consider it gut-check time; push aside the game-playing. You can jump right back into a powerful God relationship with both feet, right now. Remember, it involves your whole person: your mind, emotions, heart, spirit, and will. You know it when you have it. Begin the process of connecting (or reconnecting) with him. Go for it. Experience him.

This takes me back to when I was on the staff of Young Life working with teenagers in Bermuda. One day while just hanging out on a street in downtown Hamilton, I met a nineteen-year-old man. He looked pretty rough; his face was red with scarring from acne, and it was apparent he had been hitting the bottle a bit too much. As I got to know him, we became friends, and he eventually put his trust in Jesus at one of our weekend camps on White's Island. Weeks later, I remember him sitting near me on the floor studying the Bible, seeking to know about Jesus, and it was a great picture of transformation. Sometime later after I had moved on, I received word that he had drifted away from the Lord, which hurt me and disappointed me. But when Linda and I were invited back for a cookout in Bermuda for former Young Lifers, I was overjoyed to see that my friend had returned and was back following Jesus. Alcohol would eventually take this young man's life, but not before he had recommitted his life to Jesus.

In life I have always been challenged by what Jesus said in Matthew 10:37: "Anyone who loves his father or mother more than me is not worthy of me; anyone who loves his son or daughter more than me is not worthy of me." This says that our love for God must be so great and so personal that it will dominate our lives, making it appear that we hate our families compared to our love for him. Wow!

I know what it is to love my family. My wife and I have been blessed with three daughters. When each of them headed to college, however, my love for them was really tested. It was at that time I would sometimes wonder, "Was my love for them just lip service, or was it genuine relational love and unconditional?"

When one of our daughters broke up with her fiancé, I drove three hundred fifty miles to take her out to dinner. Over dinner she asked why I came up. I said, "I just want to tell you that I love you." She broke down and cried, knowing I loved her and would go to any lengths to show it.

Another of our daughters, in her first year of college, pulled away from Linda and me, and for a season she headed to another state more than a thousand miles away. I remember calling her after a few months to say that I would really like to come visit her sometime, and she said she would like that. I said that was good because I was right outside her apartment in a rental car. You can imagine her response, but my intent was to communicate unconditional love. I certainly don't want to leave out our other daughter, who was student teaching while dealing with a brutal case of acne. Her supervising teacher was belittling her in an abusive way, and I saw red. I drove those three hundred fifty miles to let her know I loved her. Thankfully, I didn't confront the teacher, or I might have been making my next phone call from jail.

As great as I think my love is for my girls, it needs to pale in comparison to the love I have for Jesus. I am not sure it does, though. Let's talk about this love for a moment. It starts with God loving us so much and so wanting to be in relationship with us that he humbled himself and came to earth in human flesh. Picture it: God in human flesh living and teaching the truth but coming with the ultimate purpose to die because of his great love for us. His was a love motivated by mercy and grace and sacrifice. That kind of love demands a response: a spiritual, heartfelt relationship that begins and never ends.

Love Expressed Practically

Scripturally, the Author of truth says that the best way to be in a personal relationship with Jesus is to express it in five relational actions or responses. They are not static or mechanical or meant to be on a checklist because they are relational with the person of Jesus.

No. 1: Knowing the Almighty God in a deep manner is the beginning of the relationship *he* wants.

This includes knowing a lot about him: his ways, his mind, his actions, his heart, his nature, and his essence. The Scriptures have been protected for thousands of years so that we can know him. We know that there are close to fourteen thousand New Testament manuscripts, a number far greater than copies of Greek and Latin authors such as Plato, Caesar, and Aristotle. Archeologists, such as Nelson Glueck, have great respect for the historical accuracy of the Scriptures.

When we see how God relates to people, both his enemies and his people, we know what we need to know. He does not change from day to day; he never changes. In John 17:3, Jesus says, "Now this is eternal life that they may know you, the only true God, and Jesus Christ whom you sent." This word "know" is very personal and in-depth. In some ways, this knowing is seen when Adam "knew" Eve his wife. The closest knowing-love we have as a human is with our spouse when there is a covenant commitment and the two become one flesh, including mind, spirit, and feelings. God wants us to know him deeper and more completely.

You might say this doesn't sound very much like other religions. Good, that's the point. Knowing God isn't tied to Bible trivia or tasks or meetings, but rather to the Person. Religion is rules and ritual, and it is impersonal. It is even self-centered. May God motivate us to know him better and not substitute religious activity for knowing him.

No. 2: Loving Jesus is the essence of the relationship with God.

In John 20, Jesus asked Peter—in the aftermath of Peter's denial—three times, "Do you love me?" The Greek word *agape* is used the first two times, which means *unconditional love*. It is a love that says, "I love you no matter what happens and no matter where you call me to go." The depth of this love is seen when God loves us in spite of what we do or who we are. This kind of relationship is not what the world offers or what ordinary people experience or express. It is a love motivated by God. The third time, the Greek work is *phileo*, which is the love of a friend. Jesus even calls us "friends" and laid down his life for his friends. This last of Jesus's calls for love indicates this friend love is in some ways the highest form of love. It is love of friends sticking together in battle; they go out together and come back together. They have each other's back. "Peter, do you love me as a friend loves?" To love Jesus is a combination of *agape* (unconditional love) and *phileo* (friend love) and all tied to the greatest command: Love God with all your heart, mind, soul, and strength. They are both needed to give Jesus the love he requires.

No. 3: Trust in God.
When I know God is all-powerful, all-knowing, never-changing, sovereign, etc., and when I know he loves me more than I love myself, I can trust him. He is trustworthy. We can bank our lives on him and what he says. Here is my prayer:

> You are trustworthy, oh God. You have always kept your word. Thank you that Scripture confirms that. I can take you at your word because your word is your bond. When my employees trust me in what I say and do or when my wife trusts me when I am alone, I feel elated and affirmed and blessed. Lord, how pleased you must feel when I step out in faith to trust you. It says you are worthy of all my trust.

As a father, it means so much when my children would trust me whether or not they understood me. God is pleased when we put our faith in him and trust him as God and what he says. He is reliable.

No. 4: Obey Jesus.
Jesus gives all of his commands for our benefit and out of his love for us. So when we obey him, it communicates to him in a tangible way that we truly love him. Loving Jesus equals obedience; obedience doesn't equal love. This is huge! When someone loves Jesus and truly respects him, it will be spontaneous. If we are on his team and truly he is our Lord, we will go where he is going, on the same train or in the same direction. To disobey is not only to *not* love but it is

to not *respect* the God that Jesus is. It is also possible to obey Jesus's commands and not love him; that is, doing the right things for the wrong reasons. It could be an indicator of how stale your relationship with God is or how mechanical it is.

No. 5: Praise God.
For the last component of this relationship, look at the responses of people in the New Testament when they are healed by Jesus. The first thing they do is praise God. In a moment, it dawns on the person that God is powerful and loving and worthy of worship.

> *Lord, these healed had no other appropriate response than to fall on their faces and give thanks and praise and glory to you. They know things wouldn't have worked out without you stepping in. We see who you are and your very essence, and then we experience your love. We are undone; we can only lift you up in praise.*

Having the mind of a scientist, I am drawn to logical material such as the letter to the Romans. It is well laid out, covering the essential theology. My heart is touched as well as my mind. For some reason in the last number of years, I have been drawn to the Psalms, where David is able to get in touch with his heart. I am not very good at that, but I know it is part of the way God made me. If I am going to be a whole person, I need to know what is on the inside, under the surface, and express it.

David authored many of the Psalms, and God has used them to help me go deeper in knowing and sharing my heart with him. David was a man after God's own heart (I Samuel 13:14). I want to be that man, and I encourage you to pursue that level of devotion as well, whether man or woman.

I like the fact that David was a warrior, a fighter. I fought as a younger man, and today I fight for gain in the marketplace, in athletics, in the world, and in finances. Warriors strategize, survive, and celebrate victories. When David was a young shepherd boy who protected his sheep from bears and lions, he learned to rely on God for inner strength that prepared him for battle. The battles are won between the ears as well as through the inner man. Strong leaders need strong insides.

David loved the thrill of being in a leadership role, but the responsibility scared him. As a man, I can identify with him in this area and know how he needed the Lord in those times. As a man, he was as a luster, adulterer, murderer, and a phony in his cover-up. I can identify with some of those for sure, unfortunately, but men need to draw from their walk with God in dealing with success and failure. God wants to be involved. He is right there. I like David because he was a man after God's own heart; he confessed his sin and was restored (Psalm 51). God asks of women the same thing he asks of men. He wants us to have the heart to passionately pursue him.

Delighting In God

God delights in us (Psalm 16:3) and calls us to delight in him (Psalm 37:4). All pleasure and joy and fulfillment are in him. Life is in him. Our inner longings for fulfillment and satisfaction are only met in Jesus. When you delight yourself in the Lord, you will find that God shows up in a way that no other person or thing can: He will give us the desires of our heart, which will be the desires he has for us. Psalm 63 is a great example showing the relational experience David had with God while in the desert. David earnestly sought after and pursued the face of God so that he could be with God. His soul had a deep thirst for God—to know God and to experience him. We all have tried so many substitutes for God only to find, like David, that nothing but the Almighty would satisfy.

Experiencing God's Richness

Let's look at some more times when David wanted to meet with God and experience the richness of being with him. "As a deer pants for the streams of water, so my soul pants for you." This is a clear expression on the soul to be in relationship with the living God, to meet with him and share life and truly gaze on his beauty (Psalm 27:4). David's heart yearned for the one and only God (Psalm 84:1). This accurately expresses what everyone is looking for and helps explain why we are so easily satisfied with ineffective substitutes for God, things we call idols. There is so much more in having a life that finds fulfillment in him.

Envision a woman or man meeting with God and experiencing who God is, and that being the only love that will satisfy and fulfill that inner longing?

You might be wondering: How does someone after God's own heart, as seen in these verses, slip so far away from that relationship with God that he or she moves toward lust, adultery, or murder? David was pretty good at covering the bases because he had learned to be savvy as a warrior fighting Goliath or lions and bears as well as trying to stay alive around Saul. When sex is involved, some of the best men and women compromise their non-negotiable convictions. David looked so much like the in-control king and the winning warrior until Nathan confronted him. His relationship with God won out as the man after God's own heart. Look at his confession in Psalm 51. David had the courage because he had the heart to acknowledge to God that his sin was basically against God. He hadn't loved God enough to obey him. Of course this type of behavior breaks God's heart; he grieves when someone he loves doesn't respect and honor him. As David asked for mercy, God, who is rich in mercy, love, and compassion, listened to David and desired to bring him back into fellowship with himself. When we are out of fellowship with God, the joy, contentment, and peace depart as well. The relationship is there but not the real sense of the *love relationship*.

Making It Personal

How does this address where we might be as a real man or a godly woman who desires an authentic relationship with God? Many times when we are in pain, we go to the famous words of Jesus for comfort. We should. Jesus is addressing us in our weariness with our relationship with him. On the other hand, going through the religious motions is old and unfulfilling. It's routine, impersonal, and a sham. In many ways it is just cultural, and we are living this religious experience to appease our consciences or to impress others. We don't have the courage to be real and admit, "I really don't have a personal walk with Jesus." Still, Jesus says, "Come to me, all you who are weary and burdened, and I will give you rest. Take my yoke upon you and learn from me, for I am gentle and humble in heart, and you will find rest for your souls. For my yoke is easy and my burden is light." (Matthew 11:28) Are we weary of the performance and want the real thing: Jesus?

All the way back in Isaiah 55:1-6, the call of God is there. Look at some of the phrases that reveal a longing heart for God. Maybe you identify:

"Come, all you who are thirsty . . ."

"Why spend money on what does not satisfy?"

"Give ear to me . . . listen to me . . . that you may live . . ."

"Seek the Lord while he may be found . . ."

"Call on him when he is near . . ."

God is calling you and me to an in-depth, ongoing, intimate relationship with him on a Spiritual level. Yes . . .

Lord, I am completely undone to realize you want a relationship with me, a personal one where you never leave me, a permanent relationship. For twenty-four hours a day, for seven days a week, we are in relationship. I can't get a handle on that, but I take it as fact, and I am experiencing you. I am made to need love, and Lord God, you love me, and I get to love you back. I feel a sense of joy filling me now. I long to know you in a deeper way. I long to be with you and enjoy that deep fellowship. This feels better, richer, and deeper within my soul and spirit, like no one I have ever experienced before. . . . I long to experience you in a deeper way. I long to be with you and enjoy that personal fellowship. Going to meetings, even worship services, seem so distant unless I am truly engaging you by being aware of our connectiveness and oneness. I like it when I have a sense of "as I go" in life that you are right here with me. When I pick up my Bible and read, you are there just as much as when I drive down the road in my car or when I am eating dinner with my spouse. Some of that time, I am not aware of your presence. I would be more honest if I said most of the time that I am not aware that you are right here with me. Help me talk to you as I go.

As you read this, are you aware Jesus is right there with you? Recognize his presence. Talk to him. Listen. Remember that part of having a relationship with Jesus is to know what Scripture says about him, especially what Jesus laid out in John, chapters 14-17. Meditate on those truths; take them by faith. He is saying, "Come to me and drink: let your weariness be met in me."

Group Discussion Questions:

Hook: How is "relationship" the key word for you in your life in general? Please share some personal examples.

1. Head. How can you support that the key word in all of Scripture is "relationship"?

2. Heart. How is it true that "relationship" is or isn't the key word for your relationship with God?

3. Heart. Emotions, wonder, surprise, fear, or dread might come over you when you begin to comprehend and feel who Jesus is and that he wants to know you and be in a love relationship with you. Get in touch with those feelings as you grasp this God-you-relationship. Share with the group.

4. Heart and Hand. If "relationship" is the key word in Scripture and is the most important aspect of life, how is Jesus the essence of life or as Paul says, "In him we live, move, and have our being"? Try to share with the group that experience you are having with Jesus, or share how it seems like you are experiencing it, or if you don't know how to experience him.

5. Hand. Take each of the five relational actions (know, love, trust, obey, and glorify or praise God) and share how they could be expressed practically on a daily basis.

3

Jesus Will Say,
"I Never Knew You"

"Lord, the one you love is sick."
— Lazarus's sisters
JOHN 11:3
〜

MY DESIRE THROUGH THIS BOOK IS TO BE POSITIVE AND TO PRESENT the possibility of knowing God as inviting and encouraging. At this point, though, I want to challenge you. I want to get you out of your comfort zone, maybe even cause you to examine where you stand with Jesus. Even more than that, I want to make sure you have a genuine relationship with Jesus. Too easily, we fool ourselves into believing we have a relationship when in fact there is none, or very little.

Does going forward at an event or praying a "sinner's" prayer make someone a follower of Jesus?

Dietrich Bonheoffer wrote a book called *The Cost of Discipleship*, in which he questioned the reality of being a follower of Jesus. It is normal to have easy "believe-ism" or what Bonheoffer calls "cheap grace." Later, David Platt challenged us on the cost of nondiscipleship, or what I would call nonrelationship, in his book *Radical*. These are serious charges. The reality or the lack of the reality of having a true relationship with Jesus has eternal consequences.

Most who call themselves Christians today are not disciples or followers of Jesus. Research shows that there are few, if any, differences between the believer and the unbeliever. David Kinnaman is the president of Barna Group, a survey and research organization. In his book *unChristian* he writes, "In virtually every study we conduct, representing thousands of interviews every year, born-again Christians fail to display much attitudinal or behavior evidence of transformed lives." Their vices include gambling, viewing online porn, using illegal drugs, stealing, and having sex outside marriage. In poring over the Scriptures while writing this book, I asked myself if I was just going through the motions as a cultural Christian or if I was truly in a love relationship with Jesus. What about you? I challenge you to perform a sober evaluation of yourself.

When my wife had cancer, that necessitated lots of prayer as well as surgery and chemotherapy. This experience scared us greatly. Later I had prostate cancer. After getting over hearing the C-word from my doctor, the tough part was deciding whether to have surgery, radiation, seed implant, or possibly chemo. It wasn't so easy discerning what to do. I received lots of counsel, prayed a lot, and then had to make a decision. I needed the best diagnosis I could get, as well as the best information and counsel from those who had the expertise. When it comes to whether you truly know Jesus and are engaged in a love relationship with him, you will have to do a diagnosis and come to a conclusion based on the revealed Word of God.

What most of us are hearing in church, on the radio, and through our personal experiences with Jesus is far removed from what is laid out in Scripture; it breaks my heart. If you don't know your condition, how will you know the solution? Most don't know what their condition is, let alone the solution. Platitudes about my cancer, the treatment, and even my feelings were irrelevant. Having your personal view of what Jesus said and did is useless. Truth and reality are all that matter. One reality is that most of those sitting beside you in the church pew week in and week out are not in a relationship with Jesus! Did you comprehend what I just said? You could be that person who might have prayed the sinner's prayer but you do not have a personal relationship with Jesus. This isn't about cancer. It is far more serious!

Love Greater than the Love for Your Mother

Jesus has extended a call to follow him that is radical, spectacular, and life transforming. Most people have missed it because they have been misled into following a mediocre form of Christianity that has been redefined and watered down. We've changed the meaning of being a disciple of Jesus. Mediocre means going halfway up the mountain and stopping.

Earlier we looked at the passage in Luke about hating your family in comparison to your love for Jesus. That is scary! Do you hate your mom? Even more, do you love Jesus? Wow! You have got to be kidding me. Jesus said that? Here, Jesus is explaining that one's love for him must surpass the love that one has for valued family members.

Friend, I have anxiety in writing this, but I promised from the outset to be open and honest. I honor and love my dad because he taught me to be a man, but I wasn't overly close to him. He was pretty old when I came along, and he was somewhat of a workaholic. My mother lived to ninety-one and loved me unconditionally, prayed for me, encouraged me, and pointed me in the right direction. I loved her so much, and the idea of hating her seemed out of the question. I see where Jesus is saying to keep that deep love and respect for her, but it will look weak and almost like hate compared to my love for him. You might be thinking, "I can't imagine loving Jesus like that." Guess what? That is what he is calling us to do.

To make sure we don't miss the point or think he didn't say what he said about our love for our parents, he adds spouse and children to that directive. *Oh, my goodness.* So much of my adult life has been centered around my wife and three daughters, and I truly love them unconditionally. How do I have the capacity to love Jesus so much more than I love them, you might ask? By loving Jesus with all your heart, mind, soul, and strength, he will give you more love than you can imagine for your family and others. But your love for him must be all encompassing. You need to be "all in," as they say. This is what Jesus is talking about in Luke 14:26. Go back and read it to see if I misquoted him. True personal knowledge of Jesus while bathing in his love for us will make it natural to trust Jesus and praise him. He will be our all.

Not only does God want to be the ultimate relationship in our lives, he also wants us to see that relationship as our most valuable possession. "The Kingdom of heaven is like a treasure hidden in a field. When a man found it, he hid it again, and then in his joy went and sold all he had and bought that field." (Matthew 13:44) The man understood (knowledge of Jesus) the great value of the treasure well enough that he was willing to sell everything he had to obtain this ultimate treasure. God wants us to be willing to let go of the good in order to be in on the best. This is a radical call. Just as he requires us to "hate" our family so that we will love him the way he asks, he calls us to pursue him over all our possessions.

To me, the only way to address this is that we truly see Jesus as our treasure, our first love. If we commit to that, he will show us about the rest. The focus should be on the treasure, not the selling. It is so easy to fall into the temptation of trying to quantify what to sell or not sell. However, that misses the point, which is to fall more and more in love with Jesus. In turn, he will reveal any action on how to handle other possessions. Love directed in the right direction will sort out all other issues. Trying to love two masters will only lead to anxiety and confusion.

In the South I am surrounded by all kinds of Christian activity: seeing churches on every block, praying before sporting events, quoting the Lord's Prayer, asking where friends go to church, and reading familiar captions such as "In God we Trust," "One Nation under God," and "God Bless America." Then we go to church, sing the hymns routinely, read the Bible without really paying attention, bow our heads and close our eyes only to have our minds drift off, recite creeds ritualistically, and listen to the sermon, all for naught. I hate to admit it, but I have bowed my head and closed my eyes when there is corporate prayer and have just gone through the motions . . . no heart, no real praying. I have even uttered "uh" or "yes" at the right time to appear engaged. Jesus told the teacher of the law, "These people honor me with their lips, but their hearts are far from me." (Mark 7:6). Jesus challenged those praying about it being just a show. What is the difference in an unbeliever's relationship to God and the church-goer who is going through the motions?

You Might Be a Practicing Agnostic

Part of that religious activity is to connect to nice people, evaluate the service and the sermon, check out what people are wearing, hear everyone say they are fine with a smile, and, lastly, tell the pastor on the way out what a good sermon it was. Then we go home, forget what was said, and get back to our lives. There was no new knowledge gained of Jesus, no movement to love him more, no connection as to how to trust Jesus in the future, no action, and, most importantly, no relationship with Jesus. Even though we believe we are Christians, we are actually practicing agnostics or atheists because he isn't really a part of our lives. Many of us have long been around the idea of God . . . it almost seems un-American to not believe in a God. However, a personal God and a personal relationship with Jesus remain foreign to us.

I once attended a meeting with some men's leaders—about a dozen of us. The speaker was a former pastor who now leads an organization that comes alongside churches to assist them in building the church. This former pastor said there was an "elephant in the room" when pastors meet together: they do all the right things such as prepare the sermon, present it, take up the collection, sing hymns, and wait at the door to hear "Good sermon," from the departing churchgoers but there is no *transformation*! How sad and discouraging. People are not experiencing the living God in a personal way. They don't know how to. I know a founding pastor of a church who had his PhD in New Testament, but he didn't really begin a relationship with Jesus until he was a few years into starting his church. Similarly, a friend of mine with a prominent position in the marketplace told me that even though he had long attended church, gone to a Christian school, and participated for two years in a very popular Bible study, he had done everything but receive Jesus in his life. He never had a relationship with Christ. That could be you. Living in a Christian culture doesn't make someone a Christian or guarantee any relationship with Christ.

In some parts of the country many people don't consider attending church; nor do their neighbors, for that matter. They have checked out from that habit. Church attendance is irrelevant. In

Vancouver, Canada, fewer than 5 percent of the residents attend church; they have no time for God. Many countries in Europe have even less church attendance than Vancouver does. It also appears that America is on that same downward path of destruction. We have to be countercultural by walking hand in hand with Jesus.

Personal Relationship vs. Head Knowledge

All the empirical evidence of God's existence can't substitute for our need for a personal relationship with God. Many know about him, but he is only hearsay or a theory. God seems like a good idea to many, a bad idea to others. The idea of him somehow makes us feel better while surrounded by the chaos and uncertainty of the world around us. Yet we understand him to be like a watchmaker, who makes a beautiful watch then puts it on the shelf to run by itself. Principles, rituals, activities, memberships, religious language, and crosses around necks really don't mean much unless a person is in this very personal God-human relationship. That is why God became a man in the human form of Jesus, so we could truly know him and walk with him. God is a person we can relate to in the spiritual realm as well as the personal realm. We all need to be loved and known. God is here to say, "I want you to know me and love me because I surely know you, and I love you dearly."

Job is a good example of a man who was upright and feared God, but he had a long way to go in order to really know God. After all the pain he went through with the loss of his family and livestock and, later, his experience of physical pain, he responded to the incomprehensible God by saying, "My ears had heard of you but now my eyes have seen you." (Job 42:5) This is a personal encounter. In 1 John 1:1-4, note that they said, " . . . we have heard," " . . . we have seen with our own eyes," " . . . we have looked at," and " . . . our hands have touched." The disciples are talking about Jesus and their personal contact and relationship. Jesus wasn't an icon or a bumper sticker but a person who could be known. That is the reason he came to earth.

Look at what else John is saying about who Jesus is. He is "from the beginning," he is "eternal life," and he is "life" itself. The divine and the human Jesus is right in the disciples' presence; they are connecting, relating, and enjoying fellowship with him the way God intended it to be. They experienced Jesus with their five senses by being in personal contact with him. As they got to know Jesus, they wanted to entrust their lives to him and love him and obey him and praise him. This fellowship with Jesus can be experienced by believers when we realize that is the reason he came.

After we have seen, heard, and studied about God, we are compelled to love him because of the overwhelming sense that he has given his all for us. I personally comprehend when I love my wife, and it includes words, actions, and feelings; yes, my whole self. I can't play games with her or Jesus. Someone that is so big and powerful and yet so loving becomes easy to trust because he has my best interests in mind. Even his commands are not burdensome; I desire to obey them because they are for my good, not to cramp my style. Without thinking about it or needing a hymn to assist me in prayer, I find I spontaneously begin to praise Jesus since his presence, power, and love are being poured out on and to me.

The Scariest and Most Challenging Statement Jesus Ever Made

Let's look at a challenging statement Jesus made because it will scare you. It will shake your belief foundation and cause you to look to your heart and to him for the truth. Frankly, it gets my attention. Matthew 7:21-23 has to be the toughest of all of Jesus's statements:

> **"Not everyone who says to me, 'Lord, Lord,' will enter the kingdom of heaven, but only the one who does the will of my Father who is in heaven. Many will say to me on that day, 'Lord, Lord, did we not prophesy in your name and in your name drive out demons and in your name perform many miracles?' Then I will tell them plainly, 'I *never* knew you. Away from me, you evildoers!'"**

Please notice that Jesus says, "I *never* knew you." They did some pretty spectacular things in Jesus's name for him to say, "I *never* knew you." That shows me that maybe you and I are saying, "Jesus is my

29

Lord and Savior," the right words, but we might not enter the kingdom . . . that we might not be in a personal love relationship with Jesus. That is scary! Even Satan acknowledges God in James 2:19. Lip service will not get it. Knowing the facts will not get it. It's all about the relationship, and our actions must and will show it. Going back to the passage in Matthew 7, look at what these people had been doing: prophesying, driving out demons, and performing many miracles, all in Jesus's name.

Without bringing attention to myself but wanting to put on the table my Christian experience—being a Young Life staff person for ten years (some overseas and some in the inner city), graduating from seminary, teaching Sunday School for years, serving as an elder in my church for decades, being the founder of a national discipleship ministry to men and women, authoring a two-year curriculum based on the Bible, going on mission trips to Mexico, Russia, Spain, Haiti, and Canada, and donating lots of money—I can claim lots of religious activity. From my perspective it was kingdom oriented, but how can I know if it was truly kingdom oriented from God's perspective? Maybe these activities were more about my feeling useful, trying to show God what I am doing, or impressing others with my service and dedication. Frankly it feels pretty good having done all those things. I got some clout out of it from others, and I received a "Well done, my good and faithful son," compliment from my mother. But has all this really impressed God? He is about relationships, not performance. There is a possibility that Jesus could say, "Hal, I *never* knew you. Away from me, you evildoer." Does it get your attention when he says, "I never knew you?" It does mine. You know what "never" means in the Greek? *Never!* I believe I do have a relationship with Jesus that is eternal, but it is based on my faith in Jesus and what he accomplished on the cross with his death. All of my Christian activities don't make me a believer. They are expressions of my belief and an outflow of my heart.

This is not meant to be a guilt trip, but it is a real gut check. It might be a guilt awakening that will be used to save your life. If so, I pray you will respond accordingly. The real issue at stake is how much of a reality Jesus is in your life and if this is a person with whom you have a relationship that you are passionately pursuing.

Lord, Almighty God, I feel a serious gut check coming on. Is there a possibility that you could be saying to me or these readers that you never knew us? I sure don't want to hear that at the end of my life when I stand before you, but I want to know for sure right now that we are in relationship. I know this relationship isn't based on my feelings, but on what you have done on the cross as well as in my heart. I take your word by faith; please confirm our relationship within my spirit.

We need to hear Jesus's comprehensive teaching and not slip through the cracks into easy believe-ism. Know where you stand with Jesus and grow deeper in that relationship. Let's check out the parable of the sower and the seed in Matthew 13. You are probably familiar with this parable, but have you become so familiar with it that you now gloss over it? Would you describe your experience with Jesus as being one of the seeds that didn't make it, either by not producing anything or by not having life beyond a short period of time?

Look at the four places the seed fell. The first fell on the path, and the birds came and ate them up. The seeds are gone; the birds have digested them. Gone means not alive! This sounds a lot like those who prayed a quick "sinner's prayer" and earned their ticket to heaven, only to continue living like they always had . . . out of relationship with Jesus. Yet their response will always be that they said a prayer of salvation. Who are they kidding? They have the message in the form of words and might be emotionally drawn in, but their heart is not engaged. Neither is their life surrendered, and there is no willful repentance, so the evil one comes and snatches the words away. In this case there is little knowledge of Jesus and no love for him.

The second handful of seeds falls on rocky places where there's little soil. The plant springs up quickly, but then gets scorched and withered because it lacks roots. We could debate forever trying to decide if someone lost their salvation or never had it in the first place, or we could just look at the minimal growth and lack of fruit, and confidently say there never really was any life—certainly no relationship.

Other seeds fell among thorns but were choked out. The results are similar to the first two seed scenarios. These people receive the message, but without roots they fall away when trouble and persecution come.

The last seeds fall on good soil. They germinate, develop leaves, flowers, and fruit, and—get ready for this radical result—they produce a crop thirty, sixty, even a hundred times what was sown. That is a person who hears the Word and understands it, and commits his or her life to Jesus, thus establishing a spiritual connection in which a crop, or life, flows out of the alive-seed.

This is so straightforward and simple. Do you get it? No explanation is needed, but it does take some soul searching. I am *challenged* by this. Ask yourself if your love relationship with Jesus is overflowing with an abundance of fruit that comes *only* from him. This is one way to determine where you are in relationship to Jesus. Be careful that you don't just look at results in the form of good deeds and activity.

Let's Make It Personal: Be Honest!

Would Jesus describe your relationship with him as genuine? Or personal? Isaiah in 1:18 says, "'Come now, let us reason together,' says the LORD. 'Though your sins are like scarlet, they shall be as white as snow; though they are red as crimson, they shall be like wool.'"

Evaluate where you really are with Jesus; don't play games. Jesus is offering a chance to come to him. Again, this is not meant to be a guilt trip for you but a true diagnosis of your walk with Jesus. He is waiting with open arms. Jesus said in Revelation 3:20, "Here I am! I stand at the door and knock. If anyone hears my voice and opens the door, I will come in and eat with that person, and they with me."

You might be wondering if this type of relationship is even possible. It might seem out of reach for an imperfect person. But let's look at a few men who did encounter Jesus, saw who he was, and followed him to the point of trusting their lives to him. In Matthew 4:18-22, we see three examples of men (Matthew, James, and John) whom Jesus called to follow him. In some ways the request isn't much different from the call he makes to us. We notice in the text that they left their fishing nets at once. It was immediate.

We are called to leave all that is important to us for the one relationship that is most important of all. It must be immediate and ongoing. Many times we feel guilty because we haven't literally left it all behind: our work, our possessions, our money. Nor have we made other radical changes for Christ. And the transformation hasn't been immediate either. Let's not forget that to follow Jesus is to have a relationship with him; he will show us what to let go of and when. This relationship starts from the inside and goes out.

All people want their lives built on a foundation that is firm, supportive, and stable so that it will stand up against struggles and fears. Many are confused, though, building their lives on self-interest and things that don't last. That will be destructive in the long haul. Jesus says in Matthew 7:24-27 to not be foolish but to be wise by building your life on a foundation that will withstand a tsunami because the storms of life will reveal the security of the foundation. Spiritual foundations that are "brain-deep" or "words-deep" or "activity-deep" or "nice-deep" will not last. The structure might look good on the outside, but it will be hollow on the inside and without a firm foundation. The way to that solid foundation is very narrow. Only a few take that road, but it leads to heaven and the abundant life with Jesus. The road that leads to destruction is wide, and the masses follow it (Matthew 7:13-14). Don't be "fooled" by being caught up in the crowd and their lifestyle and activity. A life not centered on Jesus is the life of a fool. The good news is that Jesus is calling us to the good soil. Let's get in that soil.

Jesus took things a step further when he challenged the listeners' good religious activity, or self-righteousness, as recorded in Matthew 6. He said that what they were doing was nothing more than a show for others to see and be impressed. Believe me, I have been there and still might be. There were three main areas of religious activity that Jesus challenged: their giving, their prayers, and their fasting. The human assumption is that anyone who does these things must be right with God. That kind of thinking comes easy for us; people are always trying to come up with ways of impressing God and others. Guess what the religious activities get someone: a brief pat on the back from men, but not from God. Jesus goes another step further by saying that you can't love God and money because you can't have two masters. Treasures have great benefit on earth, but they can't be the focus of life on earth or in the life to come. Jesus says to seek him first, and he will lead you in how to pray, give, fast, and handle your wealth within the context of your relationship with him.

Finally, Jesus confronts the people of his day who set the standard for godliness; in their minds they represented God. Frankly, I identify with them since I can have surface religion and self-righteousness that is only a show, as well as self-approval. Look at what Jesus said about the most religious people or the religious authorities as seen in Matthew 23. Be careful as you read, though, and meditate on the words because you might feel as I do, that I am looking into a mirror. Jesus told it like it was to the Pharisees, the legal experts of the law: "You blind fools. You are like whitewashed tombs, which look beautiful on the outside but on the inside are full of the dead and everything unclean."

As you read these verses, be reminded of the elder brother in the parable of the prodigal son, because he was self-righteous. Jesus had harsh words for these religious law keepers, the professional Pharisees, and they hated him for speaking the truth. He said they didn't practice what they preached because they lived their lives on public display in order to be exalted. Keeping rules only confuses those wanting to follow God as we focus on insignificant things and miss the important things in life such as justice, mercy, and faithfulness.

Are you ready to get out of the religious rat race of trying to be a Christian and instead be someone who is rightly related to Jesus in a love relationship? In Matthew, Jesus said for the weary to come to him. He didn't say to follow rules or rituals or pose or play religious games or conduct surface activities; those things leave you hollow and on a treadmill to nowhere. You can find rest for your souls! That rest translates into joy, fulfillment, and life versus routine, performance, burdens, and failure. This is the relationship Jesus offers.

Have You Received the Right Jesus?

Jesus goes on, in Matthew 9:16-17, to say we are trying to live in old wine skins: the law and our way of doing it, our system of thought, whatever that might be. Your knowledge of Jesus might be inadequate or just plain wrong. Either you have "accepted" the wrong Jesus or "rejected" the right Jesus. Jesus is saying there is a new game in town—or the new wine skins that will put us in a right relationship with him—based on truth. All other world religions are based on laws and works; only Christianity is based on faith, love, and grace. However, most "followers of Jesus" base their relationship on laws and works. They are no different from those in other world religions. Jesus said in Matthew 5:17, "I came to fulfill the law," which means he came to fulfill the law full of meaning, purpose, and relationship. We can't mix a law-based relationship and a love-based relationship, yet that's the dilemma faced by many who call themselves Christians. They claim salvation by grace, but they live a life of works trying to earn favor rather than developing a relationship with their Savior.

Jesus says, "Come to me, all you who are weary and burdened, and I will give you rest. Take my yoke upon you and learn from me, for I am gentle and humble in heart, and you will find rest for your souls. For my yoke is easy and my burden is light." (Matthew 11:28-30) These statements by Jesus are so liberating and motivating. Oh, how his heart breaks for us and how he longs to be in that love relationship: Life upon a life (Jesus's life interacting upon and with individuals), day in and day out, deep and passionate. In Matthew 16:24-26, Jesus said to his disciples, "Whoever wants to be my disciple must deny themselves and take up their cross and follow me. For whoever wants to save their life will lose it, but whoever loses their life for me will find it. What good will it be for someone to gain the whole world, yet forfeit their soul? Or what can anyone give in exchange for their soul?"

My friend, Bill Milliken, wrote a book many years ago that impacted my life. It is called *So Long Sweet Jesus*. In it he argued that we need to move on from the sweet Jesus who isn't biblical. Jesus isn't calling us to be nice little Christians, but rather that we need to encounter and engage the real Jesus who is life changing. The real historical Jesus who came from heaven desires to be in a deep love relationship with us, and that relationship will give us real life based on truth.

> *Lord, I want to walk with the Jesus who is God in human form who walked among us and is calling me to a passionate pursuit of you. I want to let go of the nice Jesus who is cultural, religious, and distant. I want an authentic personal relationship with you. Here I am; come near me.*

⤳

Group discussion questions:

Hook: What is your opinion on the statement that many Christians today are wrapped up in easybelieve-ism or cheap grace? Explain.

1. Head. Imagine being the Apostle Peter and denying Jesus not once but three times. Share your feelings and thoughts. Now imagine God telling you that he never knew you. Is it true? Why?

2. Head. If Jesus were to say to you, "I know you for sure," why would he say that about you?

3. Head. As a group, come up with a biblical view of how someone can have a right relationship with God. Can you support it with Scripture?

4. Head. What does true transformation look like?

5. Heart. Introduce or describe your mother to the group and talk about your love for her. Talk about the contrast between your love for Jesus being so great that it makes your love for your mother look like you hate her. What feelings well up inside you now?

6. Hand. Without being legalistic or braggadocios, what indications are there that your love for Jesus is genuine, deep, and personal? What would he say about you to make you believe you do love him?

7. Hand. What specific ways can you say, "So long sweet Jesus," and embrace the real Jesus?

Part II

An Intimate Relationship with the Creator

4

Oneness: God with Us

"This man welcomes sinners and eats with them."
— The Pharisees and teachers of the law
LUKE 15:2

Being One with God

GOD IS INVITING US TO JOIN WITH HIM IN A DEEP ONENESS RELATIONSHIP. I never wanted to be in ministry in Young Life or in the church. I wanted a socially acceptable job like my brothers, one a dentist and one a lawyer, or one like my successful friends. But God had other plans.

I had just completed my seminary training knowing God had not called me to be a pastor but had called me into ministry. I was driving south on I-65 in a U-Haul truck moving to Nashville to start a ministry to adults that was based out of Knoxville. I had never done that particular ministry before and didn't feel very strong in that ministry's purpose, which was evangelism with an apologetic approach.

I pulled up to my new house in the U-Haul truck with my wife and three daughters, one of whom was nursing. I didn't have anyone to help me unload the truck but I did call the Young Life office and they got three college students to help me. By the way, no one invited me to Nashville to help start this ministry called New Life, and I didn't know anyone in Nashville. I was only coming because God called me here. I almost forgot: I had to raise all the finances to support my salary and all the business expenses. I had to ask friends and family to join me in this ministry with their financial support. At the point of moving to Nashville, I had $850 per month support. Is that a definition of "stupid" or what? Or was it God calling me here?

After five months I began to think I was stupid and naïve. I even began to question if there was even a God because I had become so discouraged. I had been seeking to meet people wherever I could and share my ministry. The ministry was moving very slowly and was mainly my meeting men over lunch to just get to know them and cast the vision of what my ministry was. But there was no tangible ministry yet and no way to write success-filled newsletters to those who had invested in my ministry. I found out pretty quickly that when I mentioned to those I met that my ministry involved evangelism of their friends, it seemed like they broke out in a cold sweat just thinking about evangelism. It felt like I was running up a hill backward. Guess what? The old faithful fear of failure overwhelmed me. I replayed those old tapes from my past where I was a nobody, a loser, and a failure.

Interestingly, my birthday came along about six months after arriving in Nashville, and my wife, Linda, who does calligraphy, painted a mountain scene with my name on it along with a Bible verse and the meaning of my name. My name Hal means "strong leader." I was embarrassed and somewhat ashamed. I was stupid for getting us in this situation. The best definition of a leader is to look behind him and see who is following. I had very little ministry going on and very little financial support coming in. I wasn't a leader; I was a loser. But the verse that goes along with the meaning of my name was Joshua 1:9, "Have I not commanded you? Be strong and courageous. Do not be afraid; do not be discouraged, for the LORD your God will be with you wherever you go." I looked at that verse and thought I was misnamed.

However, fortunately, I knew how to study the Bible to some degree and I looked up the verse, Joshua 1:9 in context. God had commanded Joshua to lead his people into the Promised Land, and God would bring about success. Because he was called to go into the land,

God could command him to be strong, courageous, not afraid, or discouraged. *And God would be with him.* I asked myself, "Have I been called?" Yes. "Is God *with me*?" Yes. *Then get off your butt and get going,* I thought to myself.

I put a lot of weight on God leading us to do what he commands, and a lot of weight on him being *with us.* That is where I began to learn what I call the "with me principle." Now when I look back and see how he has led me and was with me, I know it was because he did call me and he is with me. I adopted Joshua 1:9 as my life verse.

God's Plan to Share Life with Us

God desires to be in a very personal relationship with us because of his nature and his very essence. As I mentioned earlier, the Almighty Creator really does want us to know *him*, not just the facts of his works and ways, but to know him in an intimate way; he wants a love-relationship where there is a oneness between himself and his creations. That is almost unimaginable. Throughout the Scriptures there are a tremendous number of examples of God interacting with mankind. One reason the Scriptures have been protected for thousands of years is so we could see his nature, his works, and his ways. We see this "with me" relationship from Adam to Moses, and from the prophets to John in the very last book of the Bible. Most of these relationships were at a distance or not visible to man, but some were a direct encounter. God chose to take the initiative and pursue a deep face-to-face relationship with man.

God Is in a Oneness Relationship in the Trinity

To truly grasp what "perfect oneness" means, look first at the relationship that encompasses God the Father, the Son, and the Holy Spirit. They were in complete unity in creation as it states in Genesis 1:26: "Let us make mankind in *our* image, in *our* likeness," as well as the oneness expressed in Deuteronomy 1:4: "Hear O Israel: The Lord our God, the Lord is one." In the Hebrew, "one" is plural, showing the unity and oneness in the Godhead. They are always in constant communion, each fulfilling their role as the Father, Son, and Holy Spirit. So in heaven and from the beginning, they always existed in this oneness, and now they want to bring us, their creation, into this deep relationship.

God with the First Humans

God shared a unique relationship with Adam in the garden in the fresh of the morning. In Genesis 5:22, it is reported that Enoch walked "with God" for three hundred years, and God's *Shekinah*—his glory or his presence—was with the Israelites. But this physical presence lasted only a short time; it was an unusual event, not the normal state of being. David expressed the extent that God knows us in Psalm 139:1-5, where he knows our thoughts and words before they are spoken. He is "with us" in that deep oneness. As David expresses, he can't flee from God's presence to the heights of heaven or to the depths (Psalm 139:7-10). God has precious thoughts toward each and every one of us; they far outnumber the grains of sand (Psalm 139:17-18).

God with Mankind on Earth

Get ready to hear probably the most incredible event in history. At least it is in the top three. In regards to Mary, who was made to conceive by the Holy Spirit (Matthew 1:20) and gave birth to a son, the prophets had spoken that a virgin would be with child and call him "Immanuel," which means "God with us." The "with me" principle is carried over from the Trinity to being with mankind and living among us in the flesh (John 1:14). Later we will see how Jesus is not only "with us" but "in us," and we are "in him." This is even more profound than you can ever imagine. Mankind was seeing God in human form. Colossians 1:15 says, "He is the image of the invisible God . . . " and in 2:9, "For in Christ all the fullness of the Deity lives in bodily form." In the book of Hebrews 1:2-3a, the author says, "In these last days he has spoken to us by his Son, whom he appointed heir of all things, and through whom also he made the universe. The Son is the radiance of God's glory and the exact representation of his being, sustaining all things by his powerful word."

God Came to Be with Us in Human Form

Using the best way to really communicate with man and to allow man to see him for who he actually is, God became a man and lived a daily life with us for more than thirty years. The same God who is written about in the Old Testament chose to become incarnate for a period of time, so he humbled himself and took on flesh, experiencing all that we as people experience in this fallen world. John expressed this incarnation in John 1:1-5 when he said the Word (God), who was from the beginning, was "with God" and was God in whom all were made. He came to live as a human and was the life and light of men. John later goes on to say this Word became flesh and lived among us (John 1:14). This great act of God to be born a baby and grow up to be a man had the purpose of bringing us into relationship with him. He desired for mankind to know him in an intimate way, to experience oneness with him. Earlier I referenced the Genesis passage that speaks of how Adam "knew" Eve. In one sense this is the intimate relationship that God desires for us, but on a spiritual level. We "know" him for who he is and have a love relationship with him. Becoming a man made this possible, and Jesus's atoning work on the cross completed the work.

Jesus with His Disciples

Most men like hanging out with other men to joke, tell stories, challenge one another, and have fun. Ditto for women in terms of spending time with one another, discussing topics such as family life and careers, and having a few good laughs in the process. Jesus came enjoying life and hung out with men and women from all walks of life.

After Jesus grew up to be a man, his mission included surrounding himself with those with whom he could share his life. This was so they could see him firsthand as he dealt with people in all walks of life: the sick, the beggars, the Pharisees, the hungry, his followers, and even the dead. Mark 3:14 says that Jesus called a band of twelve to be "with him," and then he sent them out to preach.

For three and a half years, Jesus hung out with these men. He taught them truth as they went through everyday life with spontaneous encounters. Life with a life; life upon a life. His life was with them. They saw Jesus reveal his emotions to the sisters who had witnessed their brother's death, and then they observed Jesus raise Lazarus from the dead. They heard him teach truths from his Father's heart that would be for all mankind, since they were transcultural. Not only were these twelve his focus—as they would carry his plan forward—but he also taught them and showed God's power to them, as in the instance where he fed more than five thousand with the fishes and loaves brought by one boy.

As Jesus walked the earth, the disciples not only saw how he treated people, dealt with evil, got hungry and tired, and even died on the cross—they began to internalize his lifestyle. They learned to be dependent on him in a similar way as Jesus was with his Father. Jesus welcomed sinners and ate "with them" (Luke 15:2). Even a demon-possessed beggar wanted to go "with him" wherever Jesus went (Mark 5:18). Later the disciples would receive the Holy Spirit to be with them and empower them.

After Jesus ascended to heaven, Peter and John encountered challenges from the Jewish authorities; the authorities noticed that these men were unschooled, ordinary men who had been "with Jesus" (Acts 4:13). Their lives were different and it came from sharing life together, not from taking part in religious activities or acquiring knowledge from religious texts. Jesus said in John 15:27, "You have been 'with me' from the beginning." All of this demonstrates that Jesus's strategy was his life impacting another's life, or as I say it, "a life upon a life" with a high level of personal contact. The incarnation wasn't just an event; it was a lifestyle—a oneness—with Jesus, and that is what a disciple of Jesus is: one who walks with Jesus.

With Jesus in the Spiritual Birth: Dying and Rising

(Author's note: In numerous cases in the text that follows, you will see some words and phrases of Scripture in italics, denoting author's emphasis.)

While this relationship was physical—God in the flesh—it became more than that. It moved to a spiritual bond unlike anything that had come before or has come since. Paul, in his letter to the Romans, speaks to the truth of what happens when a person responds to God's call and begins a personal relationship with him, or as Jesus called it, being born again spiritually from within. Paul says it this way, "We were baptized into Christ Jesus, *buried "with him"* through baptism in order that just as Christ was raised from the dead, we will be raised to a new life. We have been united "with him" in his death; we will be united *"with him" in his resurrection* (author's emphasis) (Romans 6:7).

Paul clarifies this truth in a different way in Galatians 2:20: "I have been crucified 'with Christ' and I no longer live, but Christ *lives in me*. The life I now live in the body, I live by faith in the Son of God, who loved me and gave himself for me." Paul goes on to say in Colossians 3:3-4, "For you died, and your life is now hidden *with Christ* in God. When Christ, who is your life, appears, then you also will appear *with him* in glory." Oh, the glorious relationship that is available to be with Jesus as one born of the Spirit! But whoever is united with the Lord is one *"with him"* in spirit (1 Corinthians 6:17). If we endure, we will also reign *"with him."* If we disown him, he will also disown us (2 Timothy 2:12). And God raised us up *"with Christ"* and seated us *"with him"* in the heavenly realms in Christ Jesus (Ephesians 2:6). This oneness, or "with-ness," comprises deep and rich theology. It is the foundation of this spiritual internal reality. (Author's emphasis throughout paragraph.)

Jesus with Us Going Forward

Picture going back to when Jesus was on earth teaching, knowing that in a few hours he was going to be crucified, yet laying out the game plan for his disciples. Jesus told them that he was going to leave them in order to go be with his Father. He said, "And if I go and prepare a place for you, I will come back and take you to be 'with me' that you also may be where I am." As part of the larger plan for relationship, Jesus and the Father sent the Holy Spirit, the *Counselor to be "with us"* because according to John 14:16, we would need him to carry his ministry forward, training and making disciples follow him. Jesus said, "All authority in heaven and on earth has been given me, go and make disciples and I will be 'with you' to the very end of the age." (Matthew 28:18-20) This personal relationship of oneness through the Holy Spirit is Jesus's way of dwelling with us, not just in the flesh, but in the spirit.

Just as this personal relationship continued after Jesus left earth and went back to be with his Father, our personal relationship with Christ goes on after we die. Jesus said, "I will never forsake you or leave you," in the same way that Jesus told the thief on the cross, "Today you will be '*with me*' in paradise (Luke 23:43). Wherever Jesus is, we will be "*with him.*" We will be with him because he promised to prepare a place for us (John 14:3), and we will be seated "*with Jesus*" at the right hand of the Father (Ephesians 2:6).

In a sense, there was a "grand finale of being" with mankind as Jesus appeared in his resurrection body to the two men on the road to Emmaus. Just as God and Enoch walked together, Jesus "walked along *with them*," even though they didn't recognize him (Luke 24:15). As they walked and talked, Jesus explained to them everything said in the Scriptures concerning himself. The men urged Jesus to stay "*with them*" and, consistent with his style, he broke bread "*with them.*" Once they understood what had just taken place, they responded, saying, "Were not our hearts burning within us while he talked with us on the road and opened the Scriptures to us."(Luke 24:32). Not only was this the incarnate Jesus but the resurrected Jesus sharing life with mankind in the flesh, paving the way to experience him in the spirit. That is what he is inviting us to.

Lastly, when John saw the new heaven and new earth in Revelation 21:4, he said, "God's dwelling place is now among the people and he will dwell *with them* and he will be *with his* people and be their God."

Joining with Jesus in a Lasting Relationship

Years ago I got a call from a good friend telling me that he had just met with a former fraternity brother who had picked up a prostitute the night before and now was feeling very guilty. My friend used this opportunity to try to talk with his frat brother about having a personal relationship with God, how such a relationship offered forgiveness, and that it would be a relationship forged for eternity. Unfortunately, my friend wasn't sure how to go any further with this man in terms of developing a salvation-based relationship, so he asked if I could meet with his friend and perhaps help out. I did, and the man is now a child of God.

At first, I began to take steps to help this new believer develop in his relationship with God by getting him into a church, but he refused to go to any. So, with a strong desire to help make him into a disciple of Jesus, I resorted to a Plan B which was to invite him to a men's Bible study I was starting up. I told him it would last ten weeks and that in it there would be discussion about what the Bible says about business. My friend Leonard Isaacs contacted his friend Darrell Waltrip (the former NASCAR race car driver and now an announcer for Fox Sports). Plan B worked out, and in fact these men's meetings have now been going on weekly in Darrell's two-car garage for more than thirty years, usually with about sixty in attendance. The names and faces have gradually changed over time, with everyone studying the Bible, building friendships, and seeing God work in a great way in their lives. Think about it: all it took was one man's prostitute experience that has led to thousands of lives being impacted.

That kind of relationship is offered to the world. The most famous verse in all of Scripture is John 3:16, "For God so loved the world that he gave his one and only Son, that whoever believes in him shall not perish but have eternal life." Have you ever noticed, though, the verses that immediately follow John 3:16? If not, now is the time to check them out. They will rock your boat and challenge your comfort level.

Jesus clearly says that he didn't come to condemn the world—that includes you—but rather to save it. Now listen deeply to John 3:18: "Whoever does not believe stands condemned already because they have not believed in the name of God's one and only Son." Did you see the word "already"? That frat brother who had been with a prostitute was condemned before I ever met him or talked with him. He didn't have to wait until he died to be condemned. What does that say to you?

Earlier in the chapter, Jesus said, "You must be born again."

(John 3:7). That phrase is so worn out and politicized that it has lost its deep meaning. In verse eight, Jesus states the truth in a fresh way with the phrase "born of the Spirit." That is deep. That is connecting believers to the Father, the Son, and the Holy Spirit. That is what the man who picked up the prostitute experienced—a spiritual oneness with his heavenly Father. This chapter is about that oneness with Jesus. Just in case you thought Jesus stuttered with the statement "condemned already," he says it again in a different way toward the end of the same chapter in verse 36: "Whoever believes in the Son has eternal life, but whoever rejects the Son will not see life, for *God's wrath remains* on them."

Where are *you*? Are you born of the Spirit? Can you honestly say and believe that you have a oneness relationship with the Creator, Jesus? Or are you condemned now?

Let's make this personal. Jesus is calling *you* to be born of the Spirit so that you can have this love relationship with him on the spiritual level. We become like Jesus by being with him, not doing things in an attempt to please him or imitate him. The relationship is a Life upon a life, a Life with a life, and a Life within a life! There is transformation in a believer's heart because of the work of the Holy Spirit in our lives through our association and relationship with Jesus.

I remember when my daughters would help their mom with different household chores such as cleaning the kitchen. Sure, she wanted to get the job done, but even more she wanted to share life with them so that they would sense her love and also catch the walk with Jesus. The truth is that he not only wants to be with us, but also in us (John 14:17).

Lord, I desire a love relationship where you are in me and I am in you; the invisible God sharing life with me. That is awesome. I sense that I am in the place of reality that you designed for me. I feel alive. I feel enriched with your presence and made whole. I feel properly connected to you. I feel free to be me, or should I say free to be who you made me to be. Let's get on with this life-changing process. I invite you into my life now.

Group Discussion Questions:

Hook: One of the most encouraging promises that God gives us is that he will never leave us or forsake us. In other words, he will be with us. Would a few of you tell about the time that stands out where you felt God's presence in such a powerful manner that you have never forgotten it?

1. Head. Discuss the key phrases in John 3:16; don't let familiarity rob you of the depth. "God so loved the world," "he gave his only begotten Son," "whoever believes in him will not perish but have everlasting life."

2. Head. Describe the importance of God becoming incarnate and what a spectacular event that was when Jesus lived on earth for thirty-three years. What are the implications of God being with us?

3. Heart. Picture yourself washing dishes at local rescue mission and then cleaning rooms. How does that help you get the picture of God living among us? Or maybe picture yourself living in a nursery for thirty-three years.

4. Heart. Try to express to the group how you feel about God's incredible love for you in his living and dying for you.

5. Head. Summarize the "Jesus with us" principle.

6. Hands. Picture Jesus coming to be with you in every part of your life: your bedroom, hotel room, your kitchen or workshop, at your computer, your workplace, and your bank account. In each of these, where are you asking Jesus not to be with you?

5

Oneness: Jesus in Us

"He is the one who comes after me, the straps
of whose sandals I am not worthy to tie."
— John the Baptist
JOHN 1:26

D R. MICHAEL GUILLEN IN HIS BOOK, *AMAZING TRUTHS: HOW SCI-*
ENCE AND THE BIBLE AGREE, wrote, "All told, astronomers
have concluded that dark energy comprises some 68 percent of the total universe, and dark matter about 27 percent. That
means only 5 percent of the entire universe is visible to us. That as-
tonishing revelation bears emphasis. Everything we call scientific
knowledge is based on but a pittance of what there is to know about
the world. *Ninety-five* percent of it is hidden from us." Astronomers
say that galaxies are filled with invisible exotic material they call dark
matter. Astrophysicists have found that the universe is expanding
and accelerating and the material behind the acceleration is dark
energy. Dr. Guillen is a three-time Emmy Award winner, best-selling
author, owner of a PhD from Cornell University, and a former Har-
vard University instructor. This personally helps me see that the
Spiritual realm is invisible but as real as, if not more real than, the
scientific realm. I am going to try to explain, knowing it is impossible to do so, the 95 percent—the spiritual realm that you can't see.
However, it is there.

The deepest and most profound teaching about a believer's relationship with Jesus is what Jesus said in John 14-17. While I'll try

to share some insights with you, we have to take these truths on oneness by faith. Jesus uses the analogy of the vine and the branches to communicate this truth, which we will look at later. They are presented by Jesus as revealed truth, because our finite minds can't fully fathom the depths of these truths. Even with the full counsel of God—the rest of Scripture—it is difficult to comprehend these truths; that is the fallen state in which we must live for this present time. Imagine what the disciples must have felt when Jesus washed their feet, predicted his own death, and even told Peter that he would deny Jesus. And now he is telling them what it's going to be like after he is gone from this earth. Jesus was explaining to them the future and also teaching them about this new spiritual relationship with God himself.

There are three spiritual divine facts about this spiritual relationship that Jesus wants us to hear. We need to accept them as coming directly from the mouth of Jesus, even if we can't fully comprehend them. They are from John 14:

1. **The Father-Son Oneness:** "I am in the Father and the Father is in me." (John 14:10)
2. **The Father-Son-believer Oneness:** "I am in the Father; you are in me and I in you." (John 14:20) (Begin to pray that you can get a deep understanding of this truth because it is mind-boggling).
3. **The Holy Spirit-believer Oneness:** "The Father will give you another Counselor to be with you forever—the Spirit of truth." (John 14:16-17)

Let's expand those points using Jesus's words. First, when God came to dwell among us in the flesh, people saw and experienced God right before their eyes. In John 14:7 and 9, Jesus basically says if you know him, you know God the Father. When you see Jesus, you see the Father, and when you accept him, you accept the Father. How can this happen? The Father and the Son are one from before creation and for eternity. Jesus is in the Father and the Father is in Jesus. They envelop one another, or they reside with one another at the same time. So to see and know Jesus was to see and know the Father. I can begin to accept and believe this because of what Scripture reveals in Old Testament accounts, in which God worked miraculously with his people, as well as in New Testament accounts, in which Jesus lived out his divinity by working miracles and through his resurrection. God the Father and Jesus the Son are one. The work that Jesus does is due to the fact that the Father is "*in him*" doing the work (John 14.11).

This brings us to a profound truth for believers: as we are in Jesus, we join that divine spiritual relationship. Just as Jesus is in the Father, now he is "in us" and we are "in him" (John 14:20). It is a mutual indwelling! Inconceivable! Jesus also said, "I am the way, the truth, and the life; no one comes to the Father except through me." (John 14:6) This statement is not intended to give "Bible bullets" to believers so we can tell others how exclusive we are in our relationship with God. Instead they are meant to say that Jesus is the way to having a relationship with the Father, to be "in him." As we know him, see him, and accept him, it brings us into this "in-ness" relationship. Paul, speaking to his listeners in Athens, says it well in Acts 17:28, "In him, we live and move and have our being." Without this relationship and this oneness, there is no life, only death. The life "in Jesus" relationship is a love relationship where we are loved by the Father, and he will make his home "with us" (John 14:23). The home is where there is complete freedom and peace because we are with our heavenly Father in perfect oneness. As the author of Hebrews says, "We have entered into the Sabbath-rest with God forever." (Hebrews 4:1-11)

The third point is that the Father is sending the Holy Spirit or Counselor to be "with you" because we "know him" and he will be "in you." "He will teach you all things and will remind you of everything I have said to you." (John 14:16, 26) "He will guide you in all truth." (John 16:13) And, "He will bring glory to Jesus." (John 16.14) This "in-ness" of the Holy Spirit is the life that Jesus gives.

Don't spend too much time trying to figure out these principles; take them by faith. Ask God to work in you all that he said he would. Let him flow. The disciples were blown away by these truths because Jesus transitioned from being "with them" physically to being "in them" spiritually: the with-ness to the in-ness. John 14:17 says, "You know him, for he lives 'with you' [with-ness] and will be 'in you' [in-ness]."

I think Jesus knew we could not comprehend this in-ness, nor could we figure it out. Therefore he gave us a parable or metaphor in John 15 to help us understand it. It is referred to as the vine and the branches by some. Jesus said, "I am the true vine and my Father is the gardener and believers in Jesus are the branches which overflow with fruit." How does that complex process work? Jesus as the Vine has branches or believers that are connected to him or have spiritual life in him, thus producing fruit out of that relationship. That is hard to understand, but in a similar sense, photosynthesis is somewhat like that. Plants convert light energy from the sun into chemical energy to fuel the plant's activity of growing and producing fruit. The point is that there is a union or oneness between the vine and the branches. They are connected to each other with the same DNA, which would be the Spirit. The life and character of the Vine, or Jesus, comes and produces fruit that looks like Jesus. All of this is right out of my major in college and all the way back to seventh grade science. I didn't comprehend it then, or today, but the analogy of the vine and the branches helps me get a handle on what Jesus was communicating about this in-ness with Jesus.

Jesus goes on to say that as believers we are charged to abide in him. Basically that is making a willful choice to connect to him by sharing our lives, our hearts, and our mind with him. There is real communication with him through conversation and living life together in a dynamic, ongoing spiritual relationship. Jesus abided in us (his work) and we abide in him (our work) (see John 15:4-5).

"Abiding" is an action word. Jesus is pursuing you to go deeper and he calls you to pursue him so that you can abide in him. On your part, it is an action to be taken, a willful action. We are commanded to abide and stay connected. Be proactive by meeting with Jesus. Open your heart to him by telling him where you are glad and excited as well as sad, discouraged, or overwhelmed. It is called prayer. That means the two of you are carrying on a conversation.

Even tell him you don't understand him being in you and you in him. Tell him you are taking it by faith and will cooperate, knowing that he is there. Yes, this is part of the ninety-five percent that we don't see. He will show up, or should I say, he has never left you. You are connected for eternity.

⬧

Group Discussion Questions:

Hook: Spend a few minutes talking about the 95 percent of the universe that is hidden from us and how that overwhelms you.

1. Head. There are four deep mysteries mentioned in this chapter. Talk about the Father and Son being in each other, Jesus being in us, and us as believers being in him, and the Holy Spirit being in us. What a mystery but truth!

2. Head. How do these truths expand your thinking to the point of being overwhelmed? How do they expand your thinking and possibilities for living with God in you?

3. Heart. Try to get in touch with what you are feeling now about describing this reality you have with God being in you. Does it scare you or excite you?

4. Hand. As a group, spend some time praying about these truths, asking for clarity, comprehension, and acceptance in taking them by faith.

6

Oneness: Abiding in Jesus

"Come, see the man who told me everything I ever did.
Could this be the Christ?"
— The woman at the well
JOHN 4:29
⟨❧⟩

T HE KEY WORD IN THE JOHN 15 PASSAGE IS JESUS CALLING A BE-
LIEVER to "remain" or "abide" in him. This is the love relationship God desires to have with us. It is mentioned eleven
times, so we have a proactive role in keeping this relationship vi-
brant, alive, and dynamic. The act of abiding and remaining has five
components, or what I call "Five Pillars of Abiding":

1. Abiding and remaining means *knowing* Jesus. This is more than
having the facts (and they are important), but it includes a personal
active relationship between God and a believer in three major parts:

a. Know the truth about God. A believer should pursue a deep
knowledge and understanding of Almighty God, the Trinity.

b. Know the relationship between the Trinity and a believer.
Know the fact as expressed in John 14:20, "I am in my Father, and you are in me, and I am in you." We have to take
this as fact and experience that relationship.

c. Know Jesus in a very personal, intimate manner. Life is in
him (Colossians 3:4). We live and move and have our being
in him (Acts 17:28). We passionately pursue Jesus.

2. Abiding and remaining means *loving* Jesus. The Father and Son have a love relationship (John 15:9), and Jesus loves us in the same way. He also calls us to remain in his love (John 15:5, 9-10). All of this goes back to the greatest command, which is to love the Lord your God with all your mind, soul, and strength. Paul says it well in 1 Corinthians 2:9-10: "No eye has seen, no ear has heard, no mind conceived what God has planned for those who love him, but God has revealed it to us by his Spirit." Jesus wants to be our first love (Revelation 2:2-4).

3. Abiding and remaining means *trusting* Jesus. The whole charge to remain or abide has its foundation on trusting who he is and what he said. His words are based on his character and his very being as God. We must choose whether we will step out and believe, or not. The author of Hebrews said it is impossible to please God apart from faith (11:6). Paul said in Romans 14:23b, ". . . everything that does not come from faith is sin." In Galatians 5:6b, it says, "The only thing that counts is faith expressing itself through love."

4. Abiding and remaining means *obeying* Jesus. Obedience is an expression of faith or trust in God, in what he says, and even in who he is. A believer must believe that what God commands is the truth, and it comes from Jesus, who loves us and wants the best for us. Obedience is an expression of love. From the outflow of the relationship, he will lead us as to what to do. All his laws are meant for our good and to enhance the relationship. One can keep the law without loving God, but one can't love God without keeping the law.

5. Abiding and remaining means *praising* or *glorifying* Jesus. When a believer sees what God is like and knows him personally, when he loves Jesus with his all, when he can trust God, and when that trust is expressed in obedience to God, then his only appropriate response is to fall on his face and praise God, giving him glory and recognition. God dwells in the praise of his people. Thankfulness and gratitude are essential parts of praising.

The Five Pillars of Abiding in Jesus

I am in my Father, and you are in me, and I am in you. All references are from John, chapters 14-17:

Know: 14:7, 9, 17, 15:15, 21; 16:3, 14, 15; 17:3, 7, 8, 25, 26

Love: 14:15, 21, 23, 24, 28, 31; 15:9, 10, 12, 13, 17; 16:27; 17:23, 24

Trust (belief, faith): 14:10, 11, 12, 29; 16:29, 30, 31; 17:20

Obey: 14:15, 21, 23, 24; 15:14, 20; 17:4, 6

Praise (worship, glorify): 14:13; 15:8; 17:1, 4, 5, 10, 22, 24

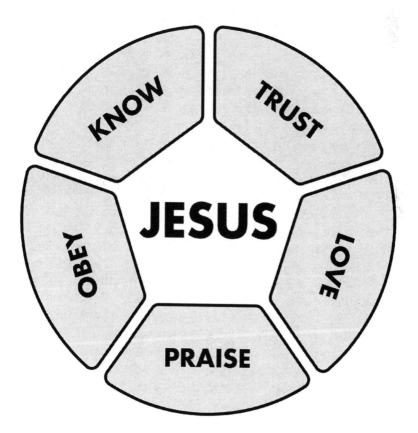

These five dimensions of abiding, or Five Pillars of Abiding, are interconnected and overlap much like a vine and a branch would. How they work together is by God's creation and his sustaining them. In a similar manner, our "with-ness" and "in-ness" with Jesus is beyond description—alive, active, and dynamic as we depend on him for sustenance and life. He flows out of us. Our abiding love is based on our knowledge of Jesus; our trust in Jesus is based on knowing and wanting to love him. Our obedience is an expression of knowing and loving him. Our praise is a response to seeing and knowing how he works and who he is as he indwells us. These five can all be functioning at the same time, such that we are aware of them, or they can be much like our involuntary muscles that work because there is Life.

Abiding, or remaining, is best expressed in these actions: knowing, loving, trusting, obeying, and praising. The life of Jesus flows in us and through us, and fruit overflows from us. Some want to make this indescribable relationship into an activity that is tangible and measurable, which can be helpful, but it can also become a source of pride that misses the relationship altogether with Jesus. This active engaging with Jesus is best described as an "as you go relationship." It is all of life, every day, all day from the time you rise until the next morning. We see David in this ongoing relationship while he tended the sheep and fought off the wild animals, and we see it some more in his alone times overseeing the sheep. Whatever life had, David was engaging the Father. This included being a warrior and a king, and is reflected in his response of confessing his sin (see Psalm 51) after committing adultery and murder (with Bathsheba and of Uriah, respectively).

We see Jesus living life in relationship with the disciples for more than three years. They were with him when he healed, when he changed water to wine, when he walked along the road, and when he prayed. It was a Life upon a life where the disciples listened, asked questions, did stupid things, ate meals together, fished, and celebrated Passover together. All was "as you go." This was living with Jesus in the normal flow of life, and that is what Jesus is calling us to do—nothing fancy, just deep and personal. Yes, the Creator and God of the universe desires to be right here with you in the midst of everyday life: interacting with your family, going to work, riding in the car, exercising, dating, eating, and sleeping.

Before we leave this topic of abiding or remaining in Jesus in this oneness relationship, let me highlight how Jesus expressed this truth as recorded in the gospel of John. It sounded so radical but true that I needed to wait to bring it up. However, it is important to address his teaching because it emphasizes the truth and experience that Jesus wants us to understand and to be in on. Jesus basically tells us that we might be looking to him for food or things that the world offers, and that we are seeking to be filled and satisfied by those things rather than *in him* (John 6:26). Guess what? Those desires are for earthly things, for "food" that will only spoil. It is no good for this life, nor will it endure to eternal life. The reality is we know this food isn't satisfying, but we continue to pursue it. Albert Einstein supposedly said insanity is doing the same thing over and over again, expecting different results. Further in John 6, Jesus said, "I *am* the Bread of Life" (v. 35), and if you eat me, you will never hunger or thirst."

Jesus describes what he means when he says that he is the bread of life, although he does so in a somewhat crass manner, as has been discussed at times over the years. He says that we are to eat his flesh and drink his blood (v. 56)! Without this, there is no life. Those in the crowd heard it clearly, and they were baffled (just as I am today). What could that mean? Was it literal? Jesus is saying to engage him at the very core of our lives by putting all our trust and belief in him, where he becomes our substance and our life. *"You will remain in me and I in you"* (author's emphasis) (v. 56). This is the mystery where, as believers, we join spiritually into the Father and the Son because in Jesus there is spirit and life (v. 63). Because this was so demanding and so radical, many "turned back" (v. 66). However, Simon said, "We believe and know you are the Holy One of God" (v. 69). That type of claim will divide and define all people, even you and me.

Our Role in This Abiding Oneness: Ask

God doesn't want to force his way on us, but he likes it when we recognize that we are poor in spirit and then call out to him for help. He desires for us to interact with him by requesting what we need and want in order to experience all the fullness he has for us. Asking puts us, as believers, where we need to be—under his Lordship. Asking means that we know him and what he has to offer. We trust him enough to simply ask because we know he is the provider. That is a form of worship.

Six times in his final sermon, Jesus calls for the people to ask of him (John 14:13, 14; 15:7, 16; 16:24, 26). Asking is essential in order to remain in Jesus. Asking is a sign of our life in his Life, showing our dependence on him. An apple doesn't ask for sap, but it is dependent on the vine, since life comes from the vine. Cut off a limb and the life source ends; death will soon follow. We must ask so that his life or Spirit can flow from us.

The real question is, what do we ask for? When I focus on the word "ask," my mind goes wild with requests. My first thought is to ask for the Cadillac, for healing of all health issues, for direction, and for help in tough situations . . . and all of these would be fine, but I don't think they are what Jesus is talking about here. It is far deeper and is tied to the message Jesus is giving when it concerns our connection to him. When Jesus says ask, seek, knock, and it will be given to you, he is speaking of asking for something deeper. He is teaching about Spiritual asking or Kingdom asking or being conformed to his image when asking. He is saying it should be about asking for the things that are important to him. He has our best interests in mind. When we are engaging in the Five Pillars of Abiding (Knowing, Loving, Trusting, Obeying, and Praising [or glorifying] Jesus), we are ready to ask for what we want. However, when we are truly abiding, we ask for the things that are important to Jesus and are on his heart. We can also ask about what is on our hearts, which is the process of being conformed to his heart and image.

The psalmist says in 37:4, "Delight yourself in the Lord and he will give you the desires of your heart." When our delight is truly in him, as we want him first and foremost because he is our life, then we began to ask for the life that is in him, the richest, most dynamic life possible. We can ask for fruit, more fruit, much fruit, and lasting fruit (John 15:2, 4, 5, 16). Having that life with Jesus will influence all we do, say, believe, where we spend our time and money, with whom we spend our time, and what we do. In 1 John 5:14, it says to ask according to God's will, and we accomplish that only when we are in fellowship or relationship with him. So we learn to pray and ask according to his will.

As humans, we are so self-sufficient that we try to do so much on our own. We pride ourselves in being independent. Remember what happened to Adam and Eve when they went on their own? In James's letter 4:3, it is stated, "You have not because you ask not." When we know God through experience and by studying the Bible, we begin to know his mind and heart and ask for those things.

Jesus takes it a step further when he says, "My Father will give you whatever you ask in my name." (John 16:23) When we pray or ask in his Name, we are praying that our request will come under the domain of all that is important to God and bring honor and glory to his name. If it is about us and our self-interests, why would our Father who loves us want to answer that request? He loves us too much, just as parents who love our children too much to give them all they ask for.

When my wife, Linda, had cancer surgery, I was a nurse to her for a solid week, 24/7 basically, almost nonstop. Mercy and service aren't my gifts or tendencies, so I had to trust God in a new way. I really began to know Linda and her needs, especially as they pertained to cleanliness, order, pain, and sleep. I did things without her asking because I knew her. I was at her beck and call. I knew her so well; I knew what to ask her for. I didn't ask her for things that were out of the question, such as, "Do you want to run around the block?" Or, "Do you want to drive to Knoxville to see our daughter?" I joined with her in what she wanted because of my deep love relationship with her. Without asking, I knew she wanted our dog, Charity, to be taken out and fed, so I did it. I managed her medications, food, baths, and appointments. I was there to serve her. Knowing her and being in relationship with her translated into actions.

In a similar way, I know God. I want to go where he is going, so I only ask what is appropriate. I ask how I can serve him. I ask what is on his mind. I ask where he is going and how I can follow. It isn't about my asking for a Cadillac. Jesus says, "You will do the things I have been doing, and you will do greater things than these." (John 14:12) We have seen this lived out with the disciples; after Pentecost, they had even more converts than Jesus did. At one point three thousand converts were added by the disciples. They did greater things over the years and covered greater distances. We just walk in fellowship, and he will open the door to what is greater. I am on his team and will go and do what he has for me. Then I will know what to ask, because I know him better.

Jesus takes appropriate life-giving asking to a fuller expression when he says this fruit-bearing life will show that we are his disciples (John 15:7-8). Abiding or remaining in Jesus will produce fruit that will look like Jesus and that will prove we are his disciples. The question is, who will this be proved to? You! Sure, others will see as well, but first it must be proved to you. You have to know in your inner being that you have life in him. Period! "His Spirit testifies with our spirit that we are God's children." (Romans 8:16)

The only way we hear and know what the Spirit says is from his voice speaking and knowing that his Life is within us, that we are alive spiritually and we see the fruit. Always know that we are in the process of becoming like Jesus: "Now the Lord is the Spirit, and where the Spirit of the Lord is, there is freedom, . . . and we are being transformed into his image with ever-increasing glory, which comes from the Lord, who is the Spirit." (2 Corinthians 3:17-8) He is doing the changing within us as we abide and remain in him.

Out of this relationship with Jesus, ultimately we give him all the glory. Eight times in this sermon (John 14:13; 15:8; 16:14; 17:4, 5, 10, 22, 24), Jesus calls believers to give him the glory. The Son and believers glorify the Father; and the Father and believers give glory to Jesus, which he had before he came to earth. And finally Jesus mentions "glory" to believers. This glory and praise to Jesus is so appropriate because all roads lead back to the Father and Son and Holy Spirit. It is all about God. All that Jesus did brought glory to his Father.

Lord, I really like these five abiding relational actions. They are personal, and I feel my heart is connecting with yours. The way I get to know you is different from everyone else, and it isn't a religious activity. Every love relationship is unique, and so is ours. Trusting you and obeying you are very difficult at times, even though when I know you and your love for me, these sure make more sense. Again I am so overwhelmed with just who you are that I want to lift you up and bless you.

"Abiding" is one of those nebulous, hazy terms that sounds good on paper but is tough to get a handle on. Begin to pursue a deeper and more real knowledge of God, and begin to thank him for first loving you, and then tell him that you love him. Without checking a to-do list, I believe you will find that you are beginning to abide with Jesus in a new and fresh way, maybe for the first time.

⤳

Group Discussion Questions:

Hook: Talk about the oneness you have with your spouse (if you are married), especially the oneness spiritually, mentally, and emotionally. Share how it is hard to explain and comprehend, but it is there (I hope).

1. Head. Talk about the five pillars of abiding in Jesus. How are they interrelated, and how is each essential? Note that there are 120 combinations. You can start with any one and it opens the door to the others.

2. Heart. Which of the five pillars of abiding is the most active in your life, and which is the least active? Why?

3. Head. Talk about the ideas expressed in the chapter on asking in prayer for the things that come out of God's heart as we abide by knowing, loving, trusting, obeying, and praising Jesus.

4. Heart. Describe your heart for Jesus. Where and when have you told him you loved him and even cried thinking about him and loving him? How is praising him one of the most human things we can do to express our humanness?

5. Hands. What would be a realistic game plan to begin to be proactive in these pillars? How can you keep them from becoming boring, routine, and ritualistic?

6. Hands. Where have you experienced joy in tough circumstances and experienced the peace of God when stepping out in faith?

7

Oneness: Jesus out of Us

"The man who made me well said to me,
'Pick up your mat and walk.'"
— The crippled man
JOHN 5:11

⌒⊱⌒

I N JESUS'S FINAL DISCOURSE IN JOHN 14, HE TEACHES ABOUT OUR ONENESS with the Godhead, where he is "in us" and we are "in him," before he moves into chapter 15, where we are called to abide or remain "in him" so that we will be fruitful. This is a very practical call to live out the oneness we have by being fruitful, which is "the life of Jesus coming out in us." Remember the tree example? The roots are the theology revealed from Scripture, and the trunk is a picture of the love relationship in which his life flows through us, producing fruit flowing out of us. We live and move and have our being "in him," and he flows out of us. The key for us is to remain or abide in him, getting our nourishment, our life, from him.

Being "in-Christ" starts with the Father being "in" the Son and the Son being "in" the Father (John 14:10-11). As believers in Jesus and sons of God, we join this "in-ness" as Jesus says in John 14:20. We are "in Jesus" and he is "in us." That is the truth, and it's a mystery. Jesus says, "I am the way to the Father." He is the way to this "in-ness" with the Godhead. By being in this "in-ness" with Jesus and to the Father, we have Truth and Life, both of which are in Jesus. Jesus takes it a bit further in John 14:17 when he says that the Holy Spirit, or the Spirit of Truth, is "in you" and "with you."

OK, that's a lot to digest, granted. Confusing? Somewhat, yes! In light of that, what does it mean when we say a believer is "in Christ"? Spiritually, it means you have joined the spiritual realm in a one-ness, or with-ness, that is beyond comprehension. This will transform a life from the inside out, as we understand this reality and begin to live it out.

There are three essential truths to understand deep within, not just from a positional point of view as someone who is in a right relationship with God, but also from an experiential one: 1) I know *whose* I am; 2) I know *who* I am; and 3) I know *where* I get my peace and joy.

First, I know "whose I am." God is my Father, the Gardener, and he has me. He initiated the relationship by drawing me to himself. I, as a branch, belong to him. Since he is sovereign, my life is surrounded—the front, the back, and on all sides—by him, and he is providentially carrying me forward because he began a work in me that he will complete (Philippians 1:6). He is in control of every aspect of my life: my future, my well-being, and my transformation. He will never leave me nor forsake me. Nothing will separate me from him. Wow! He is in, behind, and before me.

Second, I know "who I am." Since I belong to my Father and I know I am one of his sons, I have a new identity. I am a new man and a new person; yes, a new branch. The old self, according to God's view, is gone. Now he needs to be my focus, my center, and my moorings. I am not the old self I used to be, and I am not defined by all the old labels given to me by myself or by others in my sinful past because I am "in Christ," a new creation (2 Corinthians 5:17). I look at myself differently. I operate as a son, not as slave. The world, with all its glamour and trappings, doesn't define me. My successes don't define me. Human relationships are important, but they don't make or break me. Sure, it hurts when someone close lets me down. Satan can accuse me, try to destroy me, and lie to me, but I am God's child, and nothing takes that away since I am "in Christ."

Third, I know "where I get my peace and joy." In many ways, the opposite of peace is anxiety and worry. When you and I face trouble, struggles, and uncertainty, we seek peace, contentment, and confidence. We can always find it in Christ. I love how Paul phrased it when he said that he went to Troas (he had a place) to preach the gospel (he had a purpose), and had a door opened for him by God. Unfortunately, Titus didn't show up, so, Paul said, he had no peace, which I see as frustration, or maybe anger, anxiety, or worry. Paul was a proactive thinker who knew who God was and how he was in control, so he said, "But thanks to God who always leads us in triumphant procession [or victory] 'in Christ.'" (2 Corinthians 2:12-14) In Paul's struggles, the peace didn't come from the situation or positive thinking; rather, it came from being "in Christ," which means he knew whose he was (i.e., to whom he belonged) and who he was. This brought peace that allowed him to move on, knowing God was in control.

In Philippians 4:11-12 Paul said he learned that, regardless of successes or failure, he is content because of Jesus (4:13). Out of this "in-ness" with Jesus, from the beginning of his last message to his disciples, Jesus says, "Peace I leave with you; my peace I give you. I do not give as the world to you as the world gives. Do not let your hearts be troubled and do not be afraid" (John 14:27). Jesus is the Prince of Peace that Isaiah prophesied about in 9:6, the Child that was born, the Son that was given, the wonderful Counselor, the mighty God and the everlasting Father. Paul concludes in Philippians 4:6-7, "Do not be anxious for anything, but with prayer and supplication and thanksgiving, let your request be made known to God and the *peace* that passes all human understanding will guard your hearts and minds 'in Christ Jesus.'"

Where do we get our joy? In this final discourse, Jesus five times addresses believers about having joy in him (John 15:11; 16:20, 22, 24; 17:23). Joy is somewhat like peace, and both are from the Holy Spirit. It is hard to describe, but you know it when you have it. Is joy like happiness? Yes and no. Happiness is based on circumstances or happenings. It's cosmetic, based on surface needs being met or pleasure being experienced. It can evaporate in a crisis and even be faked. Joy is much deeper, as it comes from the inside with substance, and it can even intensify in a crisis. It is Spiritual and even superhuman. It is the thermostat that comes from being "in Christ" and therefore regulates the temperature. Jesus says this joy will be in you and will be complete joy that touches all of life and is filled to the fullest. He wants us to experience a full measure of his joy (John 17:13).

As Nehemiah built and completed the wall around Jerusalem in less than six weeks despite opposition, he said, "The joy of the Lord is my strength." (8:10) Sure he was elated over the wall's completion, but his joy was deeper. Paul said in Philippians 4:4, "Rejoice in the Lord, again I will say rejoice." It is about Jesus, who he is, and that he is in our hearts overflowing. We do have a role in this process, and that role is to think about the things that are true, noble, right, pure, lovely, and admirable. Put the things you heard from him into practice and the God of peace will be with you (Philippians 4:8-9). Paul sums up this inward peace and joy in Romans 14:17 by saying the Kingdom of God is a matter of righteousness, peace, and joy in the Holy Spirit. It is spiritual, deep, and beyond circumstances, our minds, and even our hearts. They are the fruits of the Spirit.

I told you in an earlier chapter about coming to Nashville where I didn't know anyone and no one had invited me. Now here's the rest of the story. About three years after arriving and meeting many men over lunch (by the way, I set a goal to never eat by myself but to initiate plans to have lunch with someone every day), I invited twenty-five men to have lunch with me. I wanted to share an idea that I had where men would meet over a long period of time (two years), develop close friendships, and study many topics relevant to being a disciple and leader of Jesus. My hope was that four of the men would be naïve enough to follow me. To my surprise, eighteen men signed up to meet for two hours before work and do about an hour and a half of preparation each week. I was truly shocked. So I started two meetings, one on Mondays and one on Fridays at 6 A.M. It had to be a God-thing because I am not a morning person. After about three months, I realized I loved these men and these meetings with them. One man commented that I had counseled him and his wife (my doctor's degree is in counseling), and I had held one of the New Life conferences in his home, but these meetings with the men were more his thing than either of the other meetings he had been involved in.

I began to explore leaving the New Life Ministry to start this leadership development ministry. As I drew near Jesus in prayer, I began to see these meetings with the men were on God's heart because we were talking about knowing Jesus better, loving him, trusting, obeying and praising him. He had given me strengths in teaching and facilitating Bible study with them. I was used to encourage friends, such as men so long for. After great counsel from friends and the peace from God, I left the ministry I was with and started Christian Leadership Concepts. I was scared to death but knew I had to be obedient. My abiding in the Vine led to starting this men's ministry that is now in twenty-one states, 85 cities, and Vancouver, Canada. The greatest part has been the fruit I have seen in transformed lives, marriages, businesses, churches, and even cities. Praise be to God!

Jesus, in John 15:1-11, calls believers to be fruitful. Fruitfulness means that there is life between Jesus and the believers, and this life is increasingly growing because of this connection. The fruit is an overflow of being in him, whereby the believers begin to show the traits and character of Jesus because we have been transformed (Romans 12:1-2) from within and now are in the process of being conformed to the image of Jesus (Romans 8:29). As James puts it, believers are becoming mature, complete, and lacking nothing (James 1:2-3), and the overflow of life in Jesus will come out in the fruits of the Spirit: love, joy, peace, patience, etc. Fruit flowing out of us means "life" within us. Live trees produce fruit because there is life within. In the same way, spiritual fruit is a sign of life—Jesus's life!

Fruit production—as expressed by Jesus in John 15—can range from being nonexistent (v. 2 no fruit) to being fruitful in a progressively growing manner. It goes from producing fruit (v. 4) to more fruit (v. 2) to much fruit (v. 5, 8) to lasting fruit (v. 16). It is important to notice in Galatians 5:22 that there is one fruit (singular) of the Spirit with nine expressions—for example, love, joy, peace, and patience. These are overflowing. Growth and fruit production in a believer are much like an apple growing, in which all parts of the apple grow proportionally and simultaneously. The peel grows at the same rate as the seeds and the pulp. Therefore, the fruit of the Spirit will be produced from within at the same rate, since there is only one fruit. A healthy believer in Jesus has great potential to overflow with the life of Jesus in an abundant way. Draw near him, grow in him, and abide in him. As a result, kingdom things will happen on this earth.

The branch or believer must be connected to the Source of Life or the Vine; otherwise, there will be no fruit. In fact, the Gardener will either cut off the branch because it is not bearing fruit or he will trim the branch to make it more fruitful. Believers can't produce fruit on their own; in fact, they can do nothing that would reproduce the life of Jesus in their lives (John 15:5). The religious— and again, this could be you—person's tendency is to live with a checklist or manmade routines that have no real meaning or real connection with Jesus. Jesus encountered this with the adulterous woman at the well, where she was trying to appear religious through religious activity and tradition with no heartfelt love or relationship with God, all lived out in a tangible world that she could manage. Jesus was saying that we must worship him "in spirit and in truth."

Life begins in believers when the Word spoken by Jesus cleans them (John 15:3). This cleansing is the work of God in an unbeliever's life to establish a relationship with him (John 6:44). The Word connects believers to God, keeps them on track, and points them in the right direction when they get off track. In 2 Timothy 3:16-17, Paul says, "All Scripture is God-breathed and is useful for teaching, rebuking, correcting, and training in righteousness, so that the servant of God may be thoroughly equipped for every good work."

I must ask where you are in this abiding and fruit producing. I often ask that of myself as well. There are really two kinds of "believers." One believer produces fruit and one doesn't. The one that doesn't produce fruit probably isn't a believer after all. Healthy, alive apple trees produce fruit. If there is no fruit, maybe there is no life on the inside. You may be familiar with sucker shoots. They can sprout from the side of a fruit tree but the gardener prunes them by chopping them off and then throws them away. Jesus says in John 15:5, "... apart from me you can do nothing," meaning producing fruit and eternal things. Why? There is not a Spirit connection. Maybe it is back to what Jesus said: "I never knew you."

Judas, one of Jesus's disciples, hung out with Jesus for more than three years where he saw miracles and heard great teaching about life and God, but he was notorious for betraying Jesus. Jesus said, "If you do not remain in me, you are like a branch that is thrown away and withers and is picked up and thrown in the fire." (John 15:6) You decide if Judas was thrown away. What about you?

My good friend and former co-worker, Mark Arnold, told me about when he was in high school and announced one night at dinner that he had prayed to receive Jesus as his Savior. His three brothers and mother rejoiced with excitement. His dad said, "We will see." Would there be a change or internal transformation that would produce fruit? Good question. I am here to say yes, that his life did change and is changing.

⟶

Group Discussion Questions:

Hook: Tell about when you first committed your life to Jesus and about the fruit that came out of your life, or didn't.

1. Head. Take some time to get a deep understanding of John 14:10 and 14:20. This could be called the "in-ness" principle. Is there an example that would help?

2. Head. Do the same thing with John 14:16-17 with the Holy Spirit. How does the idea of dark energy and dark matter help you accept this truth? Is there a better way to comprehend this deep fact?

3. Heart. What feelings do you have of being "in" Jesus and he "in" you?

4. Heart. Share your understanding and excitement of knowing "whose I am" and "who I am." Can you give some examples to express these?

5. Hands. Share examples of where you have seen peace and joy in others and yourself during tough situations. How about in celebratory situations?

8

Oneness with
Our New Family

*"Were not our hearts burning within us while he talked
with us on the road and opened the Scriptures to us?"*
— The two men on the road to
Emmaus after Jesus's resurrection
LUKE 24:32

⤺

C HANCES ARE YOU HAVE EXPERIENCED SOMETHING PAINFUL IN-
VOLVING one of your relationships with a loved one—maybe
a sibling, a parent, or a very close friend—whether it was
brief or over an extended period of time. For many of you, the relationships mentioned in this chapter will remind you of the pain you
are in or have been in.

These relationships are designed by God to meet some of our
essential and basic needs. Family is the place where personalities
and self-images are forged. It is where we are nurtured, trained, and
where we develop our morals and values. Ideally we experience what
it means to be loved and to love. We learn to accept our uniqueness
as well as accepting others. Families are where we feel at home, our
nest: a place we can always come and be at peace. If you aren't experiencing those things on earth, God invites you to experience them
with him. We all need a godly Dad and we are blessed if we have
siblings, parents, and a spouse and children.

"Relationship" is a key word in Scripture and all of life. Right relationships bring the greatest reward, satisfaction, and fulfillment.
Likewise, broken or fractured relationships can induce the greatest

pain. In many ways these four relationships I will discuss are essential, life-changing relational realities that God designed for believers, but you will miss the powerful truth if you only let them be a metaphor. I encourage you to accept them into your own life in a real way, not just hypothetical. They really describe the actual relationship that exists between the Creator and his family. In fact, they are realities that help shape and define who you are and how you relate to Jesus, as well as to all other people in your life. These four divine-human relationships (Father-son/Father-daughter, Friend-friend, Brother-brother/Brother-sister, Bridegroom-bride) will also address the relationships you have with others and vice versa: these human relationships will assist you in understanding what God has planned for you. Those without a positive relationship with an earthly father or sibling can go right to the Godhead to receive the blessing. A quick note here: upper-case references in these hyphenated relationships (Father, Son, Brother, etc.) refer to the divine; lower-case to humankind.

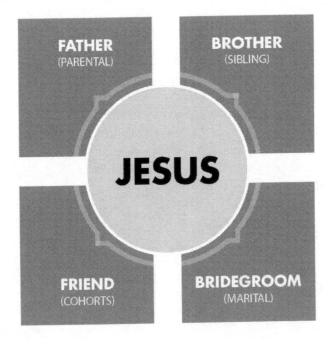

The Father-son Relationship

(This applies to Father-daughter as well)

Your personal experience with your earthly father can be very significant, or it can be one that has been painful and distasteful. Many adults have a father-wound that has impacted their lives. I don't ask you to shove that painful relationship under the rug, but I ask you to not let that bad experience define what God wants for you. You will probably look at God the Father through the lens of your father-son or father-daughter experience. That can't be helped, but I encourage you to let Scripture speak louder than your experience. Let the revealed Word of God that is based on his character give you the foundation you need and that he offers. Don't miss out on this powerful and special relationship and family.

Thinking of the father-child (son or daughter) relationship, I remember a story I heard many years ago about a prison inmate who inquired at the commissary about the availability of a Mother's Day card. There were some available, but hundreds had to be ordered because of the many inmates who wanted to send a card to their mother. In response, the prison officials decided to stock up on Father's Day cards as that day approached. To their surprise, very few sold. As one counselor at the prison said, "Most men in here 'kill' their dad daily, bury him, and dig him up the next day to kill him again, all because of the pain they experienced." If that is similar to where you are, I have good news for you: God wants to be the good loving Father you never had.

Fortunately, I had a very good father, although he was a bit older than most of my friends' dads and had that workaholic bent I mentioned earlier. When I began this personal relationship with Jesus at the Young Life camp, it told me who I am. More than that, though, it told me who God is and what he can do with a person like me. He can take a broken person and do in them what he wants. With me, he has taken an ordinary person and worked through me in an extraordinary way. All of this happened after I realized who God said I was in Jesus. He said that, as a believer, I was now a son of God, and he was my Father. My whole identity changed from being a loser (or slave, according to Romans 8:15-16) to a son. I continue to marvel that God is my Father. It was a major paradigm shift. Being one of God's sons motivated me to live out who God said I was.

The Bible addresses the fact that believers are in the Father-son or Father-daughter relationship. Let's talk about that. If you have or had a difficult relationship with your father, it's painful because your dad was probably one or more of these things: absent, distant, abusive, or perhaps nonexistent. Maybe his harshness, anger, or control is all you remember, or perhaps it was even sexual, physical, or verbal abuse. If that was the case, professional counseling might be in order, in addition to acquiring a proper understanding of the biblical view of God.

If you don't have the father-wound, you might only perceive God as big, powerful, and unknowable, especially with the way the Bible describes him as all-knowing, all-powerful, or omnipresent. This great big God seems impersonal and infinite and has always existed. He was never created, he is perfect, and he calls himself the "I Am," which says he can't be defined, even with his characteristics and essence. Yet all people are limited in their ability to perceive or define God. If we give ten descriptions that are correct, we will still fall short in defining him. He is indefinable. That is one reason Jesus came, so that we could know God in a personal way.

Jesus referred to his Father in an endearing manner when he was at one of the toughest points in his life, right before he was crucified. This endearment was evident as he was praying, asking the Father to let this experience of the cross be avoided: "My soul is overwhelmed with sorrow to the point of death." (Mark 14:34) Then going a little further, he fell to the ground and prayed that, if possible, the hour might pass from him: "Abba, Father," he said, "Everything is possible for you. Take this cup from me. Yet not what I will, but what you will." (Mark 14:35-36) Notice he called his Father, "Abba, Father" which is a very personal title and exclusive to the Father-Son relationship, which always should communicate warmth and respect.

Jesus came into the world to offer all believers this personal Father-son or daughter relationship. In John 1:12-13 it reads, "Yet to all who did receive him, to those who believed in his name, he gave the right to become children of God—children born not of natural descent, nor of human decision or a husband's will, but born of God." Yes, you and I can become children of God and have that personal relationship with our heavenly Father. Paul lays it out very clearly in Galatians 4:4-6 by writing, "But when the set time had fully come, God sent his Son, born of a woman, born under the law, to redeem those under the law, that we might receive adoption to sonship. Because you are his sons, God sent the Spirit of his Son into our hearts, the Spirit who calls out, 'Abba, Father.'"

"Adoption" is a legal term that establishes placing a new child in the family of the adopting parents, and the child has full rights, just like a naturally born child. Adoption is accounted for in Ephesians 1:5. It is overwhelming to think we have access to that infinite, perfect, eternal Creator. We can even address him as *Abba*, Father, which is a title that only comes with knowing Jesus.

At the time Paul was communicating this truth, adoption was basically unheard of. "Father" is used about ten times in the Old Testament, but never in a personal family way. We can approach God the Father face-to-face as one of his sons or daughters and call him Daddy or Dad or Papa. As Paul describes to the Romans in a letter, which is the greatest treatise on the gospel anywhere, he includes this Father-son relationship as seen in Romans 8:14-16: "For those who are led by the Spirit of God are the children of God. The Spirit you received does not make you slaves, so that you live in fear again; rather, the Spirit you received brought about your adoption to sonship. And by him we cry, 'Abba, Father.'" The Spirit himself testifies with our spirit that we are God's children. We are clearly no longer slaves but sons and daughters. Did you get that? His children!

Just as many of us have human fathers who have disappointed us, we as children have disappointed our heavenly Father by neglect or rebellion. To me, a real look into who our Father is and how he responds to us as children is seen in the parable that Jesus gave concerning the Prodigal Son. As Tim Keller points out, "prodigal" means spending money and resources freely, recklessly, and wastefully extravagant. In the story there is a prodigal father who "spends" or expresses love in an extravagant way. The youngest son had asked for his inheritance so that he could go live his life as he wanted. He did just that by squandering it on the things of the world so that he ended up living and eating with the pigs. All this greatly hurt and disappointed his father.

Fortunately the son decided to come home, and as he approached the house, the father spotted him: he had been expectantly looking for his son. With deep compassion and throwing all his painful feelings behind him, the father ran to meet the son, smothered him with hugs and kisses, and welcomed him home. "The son said to him, 'Father, I have sinned against heaven and against you. I am no longer worthy to be called your son.'" (Luke 15.21) The father not only gave the son hugs and kisses but honored him by giving him a robe of honor, a ring of authority, and sandals for his feet, and then threw a big party to celebrate his coming home. The son, the family member, returns. Awesome! This is a picture of a prodigal or extravagant loving father! That is the same response and welcome we *always* get from our heavenly Father because of our sonship.

In Hebrews 12:5-11, the author speaks to how the love of an earthly father and the heavenly Father is demonstrated in his discipline. In verse 5 it says, "My son, do not make light of the Lord's discipline, and do not lose heart when he rebukes you, because the Lord disciplines those he loves, and he punishes everyone he accepts as a son." There are two important phases here, "discipline those he loves" and "accepts as a son." Aren't these powerful? Sonship, love, and discipline go hand-in-hand when administered in the proper manner. Discipline isn't pleasant at the time, but it is for our good, and it produces a harvest of righteousness and peace. Thank God and your parents for caring enough to discipline you. Bring to God your painful experiences you had with your father, and now let God love you well.

Father, just to call you Father and for that to be a reality is hard to capture in my mind and heart. It makes you feel so close and real and personal. You not only bring yourself to our relationship but bring all your wisdom and truth and power. You are so big but yet so close. You are right here with me. I am in awe of you but so grateful you have invited me in as one of your children.

The Friend-friend Relationship

"What is a friend? It is a person with whom you dare to be yourself. Your soul can be naked with him. He seems to ask of you to put on nothing, only to be who you are. He does not want you to be better or worse. When you are with him, you feel as a prisoner feels who has been declared innocent. You do not have to be on your guard. You can say what you think, so long as it is genuinely you. He understands those contradictions in your nature that lead others to misjudge you. With him you breathe freely. You can avow your little vanities and envies and hates and vicious sparks, your meanness and absurdities and, in opening them up to him, they are lost, dissolved on the white ocean of his loyalty. He understands." (Author unknown)

"Greater love has no one than this, that someone lay down his life for his friends." Jesus not only said this in John 15:13, but he carried this out on the Cross. The greatest act and symbol of a friend is Jesus dying on the cross for his friends. Yes, God Almighty, the Creator, came to live on the earth in a human body and then gave up his life for mankind. Keep in mind Jesus, who is God, is never to be just a buddy. It is *he* who calls us his friend, and we have no other choice but to honor and worship him while joining in on the friendship he offers.

Friendship has been one of the foundational truths of my life. I love to hang out with friends; I was introduced to Jesus by a friend, and Jesus is our Friend. Someone told me once I was the richest man they knew. I asked why. He said it was because of my many friends. Because I have initiated to have thousands of lunches with men, I have had many times of being ministered to and many times ministering to them. I can truly say I feel more built up by them than I have built them up. I've gone on fishing trips to the boundary waters of the USA and Canada. I've pedaled close to twenty thousand miles with friends on bike trips, some one hundred miles in a day, across Tennessee, the Pyrenees, and

Maine. I have stood with men and they have stood with me through tough issues. I have befriended men going through divorce, bankruptcy, adultery, getting fired, addictions, manslaughter, job seeking, deaths, and many failures. We have gone out together and come back together.

Jesus came to live among us, and he selected a small group of men to be his followers, to be in his inner circle as friends. Even in that small group he had a few that were his closest intimates. First of all, Jesus takes the initiative as a friend by calling these twelve to come join him. Friends challenge their friends to go to higher ground to reach their potential and take on endeavors that are far beyond what they ever dreamed of achieving. Jesus even took Peter, James, and John with him to the Mount of Transfiguration so that they could see him in a different light and get a picture of the future. When Peter confessed that Jesus was the Christ, Jesus spoke definition and direction onto and into Peter. He saw great potential and leadership, so he called Peter forth to be just that—a leader with conviction.

He liked to get into the company of his friends to just hang out, share life together, laugh, think, and be stretched. In Mark 4:35-41 he went fishing with his disciples, and in John 2 he went with his mother to a wedding of a friend to celebrate and bless the couple. He was most accessible, and not just to his disciples. Even in Luke 15:1-2, it is recorded that tax collectors and "sinners" gathered around to hear him. Critics said of Jesus that this man welcomes and eats with them.

Dr. Henri Nouwen, a Dutch Catholic priest, professor, writer and theologian, expressed it well in his book *Gracias!: A Latin American Journal* (Orbis Books: Maryknoll, New York, 1983, pages 147-148):

> More and more, the desire grows in me simply to walk around, greet people, enter their homes, sit on their door steps, play ball, throw and be known as someone who wants to live with them. It is a privilege to have the time to practice this simple ministry of presence. Still, it is not as simple as it seems. My own desire to be useful, to do something significant, or to be part of some impressive project is so strong that soon my time is taken up by meetings,

conferences, study groups, and workshops that prevent me from walking the streets. It is difficult not to have plans, not to organize people around an urgent cause, and not to feel that you are working directly for social progress. But I wonder more and more if the first thing shouldn't be to know people by name, to eat and drink with them, to listen to their stories and tell your own, and to let them know with words, handshakes, and hugs, that you do not simply like them, but you truly love them.

Jesus had a special way of being with people and being a friend to them. In one incident he encountered a man with leprosy and, because he cared, he healed the man, thus showing he wasn't interested in being a friend for self-serving goals, but rather he befriended them because they were valuable and worth spending time with. He had the unique ability to have a balance of steel and velvet, or truth and love. For example, in Mark 8:33, Jesus rebuked Peter for talking about the way he would die, but he stood by Peter and the other disciples when the Pharisees were attacking them for eating "unclean" food. He also didn't shame the disciples when he entered the room to get in on a discussion on who was the greatest, but instead he used it as a time to teach on being great by having faith like a little child (Mark 9:33-37). That is a friend: loving unconditionally and spurring one on to more.

Let's look at three of the greatest acts of friendship Jesus had with people he knew well and loved well. The first is Lazarus and his sisters, from John 11. When Mary and Martha heard that their brother was sick, they went to Jesus saying, "Lord, the one you love is sick." This is similar to what Jesus felt in Matthew 9:36, "When he saw the crowds, he had compassion on them, because they were harassed and helpless, like sheep without a shepherd."

Later, in John 11:33-36, Jesus wept with Mary and Martha. It was a deep grief, an overflowing of love and compassion. In the second great act of friendship, Peter was the only one to say "no" to Jesus by denying him three times, and it broke his heart when he realized it. The good news is that after Jesus's resurrection, he was eating fish with the disciples (another picture of friendship by hanging out on the beach together), when he asked Peter three times if Peter

83

loved him. Jesus used two different words of love; one was unconditional love and the other was brotherly love. Jesus was looking for
Peter, his friend, to love him back the way Jesus loved him, which
was a combination of unconditional brotherly love (John 21:15-17).

In a third act of friendship, Jesus invited his main three disciples
from his inner circle to come pray with him and stand with him
when he was in the garden before he was crucified. He was deeply
distressed and troubled and asked them to come to watch and pray
with him, thus showing he wanted them as friends even though they
had let him down (Mark 14:36).

Following is an excerpt I found nicely appropriate for this discussion on friendship. It was written by Henri Nouwen and is from
the book *Here and Now: Living in the Spirit* (The Crossroad Publish-
ing Company: New York, 1994, page 19):

> It is a special occasion when friends celebrate your birthday with
> a card or a gift or a surprise party. These say I value you as a per-
> son and as a friend. I want to celebrate you. Celebrating a birthday
> reminds us of the goodness of life, and in this spirit we really need
> to celebrate people's birthday every day, by showing gratitude,
> kindness, forgiveness, and affection. These are ways of saying: 'It
> is good that you are alive; it's good that you are walking with me
> on this earth. Let's be glad and rejoice. This is the day that God
> has made for us to be and to be together.' Just to think Jesus cel-
> ebrates you as his friend.

Jesus calls each of us, as one of his followers, into a deep
friendship with himself. This is great news because we are made
to be in relationship with friends on a human level but also with
Jesus. In fact, we need both the friendship with Jesus and other
people. Stu Weber's *Locking Arms* is a great book on male friendship, but many of the points he makes apply to the friendship we
can have with Jesus.

Weber says there are four components to a great friendship,
which are applicable to men and women. The first is acceptance:
truly Jesus accepts us right where we are, unconditionally. He knows
all about us and loves us even when we were his enemies. Someone
said there is nothing we can do to cause God to love us more and

nothing to cause him to love us less. Isn't that freeing to know we are accepted just for who we are right now? However, he loves us too much to let us stay where we are.

The second trait Weber uses is affirmation. There is no one who affirms us more than Jesus. He recognizes who we are and what we have done. He also affirms us as to what we can be by seeing great potential in each of us.

Thirdly, he cares enough to keep us accountable to the standard we set as well as the ones he set for us. He will give us all we need through his Spirit to empower us to be all we can be.

Finally, he has authority over us since he is our Lord. Gratefully, he cares enough to confront.

I really get excited over Jesus calling me "friend." I love it when anyone calls me friend because it is the highest compliment and affirmation I can get. Then Jesus says I am his friend. That is rich. It causes me to feel so free to just be me, to expose myself because I feel so loved and so protected and safe. My deepest fears and shame can be revealed, and still I know he loves me and wants to be my friend. All of us have had friends desert us or talk behind our backs, but I can say Jesus has only stood with me. I can cry and I can feel him weeping for me. I feel right at home with him and can invite him into every room in my house. Ultimately, I am undone and elated to know that as a friend he has done the greatest act of love—laying his life down for me.

Jesus, I want to be your friend! I want and need you at my side. I want to draw closer to you and lay my life down for you.

Weber tells a story of a harrowing car ride with his wife through the Swiss Alps on a narrow and icy road. At one point on the journey, his wife tells him that their speed is too fast for the winding, downward slope. As he tapped the brake, the car went into a slide toward the mountain edge. Had it not been for a sturdy, steel guardrail, they would have plummeted thousands of feet below. He was thankful that the guardrail saved their lives instead of having an ambulance pick them up at the bottom. That is the Friend that Jesus is as he gives us guardrails as commands to avoid problems, but also he is the ambulance who picks us up at the bottom. What a Friend we have in Jesus.

The following is an excerpt from an article entitled "Friendship," written by Fredrick Buechner, and which appears as Article 53 in the book *Whistling in the Dark: A Doubter's Dictionary* (Harper-Collins Publishers: New York, 1998):

> There are many ways people get to be part of each other's lives like being related to each other, living near each other, sharing some special passion with each other like jogging, but though all or any of those may be involved in a friendship, they are secondary to it. Basically your friends are not your friends for any particular reason. They are your friends for no particular reason. The job you do, the family you have, the way you vote, the major achievements and blunders of your life, your religious convictions or lack of them, are all somehow set off to one side when the two of you get together. If you are old friends, you know all those things about each other and a lot more besides, but they are beside the point. Even if you talk about them, they are beside the point. Stripped, humanly speaking, to the bare essentials, you yourselves are the point. The usual distinctions of older-younger, richer-poorer, smarter-dumber, male-female even, cease to matter. You meet with a clean slate every time, and you meet on equal terms. Anything may come of it or nothing may. That doesn't matter either. Only the meeting matters.

After reading this, I trust you, too, have a sense of awe as well and are ready to exchange a high-five. I feel this when I have been around someone who is well-known. I remember meeting Billy Graham, as well as Bill Bright, the founder of Campus Crusade for Christ. Dr. Bright was the greatest visionary I have ever seen, yet he was so personal and humble. Likewise, God calling me a friend is so undoing and profound. This motivates me to respond back with love.

Growing up as a young boy, I remember singing in my fifth-grade Sunday school class the following hymn every week. It was either the only one the teacher knew or maybe it meant something very personal to him. Many commented on how bad it sounded but it left an impression on me to this day. Jesus is a friend or the Friend I want and need. This friendship theme is in many hymns to communicate this rich, abiding friendship that isn't the casual buddy-buddy kind."

"What a Friend We Have in Jesus"
(Joseph M. Scriven, 1855. From *Hymns for the Family of God*.
Paragon Associates: Nashville, Tennessee, page 466)

What a Friend we have in Jesus, all our sins and griefs to bear!
What a privilege to carry everything to God in prayer!
O what peace we often forfeit, O what needless pain we bear,
All because we do not carry everything to God in prayer.

Have we trials and temptations? Is there trouble anywhere?
We should never be discouraged; take it to the Lord in prayer.
Can we find a friend so faithful who will all our sorrows share?
Jesus knows our every weakness; take it to the Lord in prayer.

Are we weak and heavy laden, cumbered with a load of care?
Precious Savior, still our refuge, take it to the Lord in prayer.
Do your friends despise, forsake you? Take it to the Lord in prayer!
In his arms he'll take and shield you; you will find a solace there.

Lord, being an extrovert, I have valued friends so much over the years and I get energized by being with them. Some days it feels like we are going through life together much like when I am riding on a bicycle with a buddy. I feel energized by being in your presence. Having fun, thinking out loud, recognizing who you are and that you want to be with me is relaxing and fulfilling. Let's do more together.

The Brother-brother or Brother-sister Relationship

In some ways having two older brothers and a younger sister had its downside, as I have mentioned, but the benefits of having siblings far overshadow the disadvantages. For those who have no siblings, this could be great news for you as you engage and comprehend that Jesus is not ashamed to call you brother or sister. He wants you to experience all the benefits in him as your big brother that you haven't experienced on earth.

With my brothers, I see them as pacesetters for me: Joe was four years older and Morris was two years older. Joe, in many ways, was my hero. He was always bigger, stronger, and knew more about life.

He got to do things I could only hope for one day. There was a gap in our ages and experiences. So he really was my hero, especially in football. I was so proud to watch him play. I remember running out on the field after the game to congratulate him, only to find he had gotten his front teeth knocked out. Not only was he my biggest fan, but I loved it when he came to my practices to "coach" me.

The thing I remember most clearly, and which had the biggest impact on my life, would set the course of my life in a whole new direction—one of hope and a future. Sometime after I had flunked out of the University of Tennessee, I was in California wondering what my future held, feeling hopeless and full of shame. My brother, Joe, and his wife, Mary, wrote me a letter that said, "We believe in you and we think you can go to medical school." At the time Joe was in dental school. He believed in me when no one else did. My mother was extremely positive, but I heard her saying nonverbally, "Hal, you don't have what it takes." My brother set the pace after his hard times at college and then he became very successful in dental school. But more than that, he believed in me. In a sense he gave me mercy and grace as Jesus does, but in the form of words. The tongue has the power of life or death (Proverbs 18:21), and Joe's words were life to me. He helped me set a new pace for my life when he encouraged me to go back to college. I did and I succeeded but thankfully not as a dentist, in part because he believed in me as one brother respects the other.

My other brother, Morris, was more my friend who stood with me as I moved from a boy to a man. His role in my life might not have been as obvious as Joe's, but they were still important in its own way. Morris was a pacesetter socially as I began to check out the girls, and a bit later as I pursued the fraternity life in high school and college. Morris and I were in the same fraternities together. He helped me know how to dress and act. We did a lot together and even fought each other (nothing too serious), as brothers are prone to do.

I am a big brother to our only sister, Annette. What a privilege in being the big brother to her like our big Brother, Jesus, is to us. Today we live in the same city, and my wife and I love to share our life with her and her husband, Walt, from the perspective of a couple who seek to follow Jesus. As a couple we are each other's best counselors. She has been the sister-friend who sticks with me in success or failure.

When I think back to when I was a high school senior, there were a few times when I didn't want my little sister hanging around, although deep down I was proud of her and would do anything to protect her. I clearly remember in physical education class when I wrestled the boy she was dating. In my memory I pinned him in a short time with as much roughness and toughness as I could come up with to send him a message: I would protect Annette at any cost. Later when she graduated from college with a degree in interior design and started her own interior design business, I drew from all I had learned from my business experience and what I saw in Scripture to provide insights to her on running her business. In spite of my "big-brotherly wisdom," she did well.

There was a song written many years ago and sung by many that captures the uniqueness and benefit of having a brother. It isn't as rich as what Jesus is saying but it does state some of the elements of brotherhood. It causes me to value and appreciate what I have in my siblings and even with my big Brother Jesus. As the lyrics from an old song by Bobby Scott and Bob Russell say, "He ain't heavy; he's my brother" and goes on with, "The road is long with many a winding turn that leads us to who knows where. But I am strong, strong enough to carry him." Jesus is the one doing the heavy lifting, for the benefit of all of us.

I am privileged to have twin grandchildren: a grandson and a granddaughter. It has been fun getting to know them and sharing life with them. I remember observing them as siblings, literally from day one, when they came down the hallway in what looked like a portable incubator. One just lay there quietly, while the other one looked around at all the details. Their personalities have remained so different, even now that they are teenagers. The part that has been so special is observing how they interact with each other and how they are on each other's team. Sure, they fight and disagree at times, but generally they communicate in a profound manner. They rejoice or hurt with the other. Just two days ago, my grandson, Isaac, wrote a song and played it on his guitar. That was awesome seeing and listening to that, but what really stood out to me was seeing his sister, Hallie (wonder where she got that great name), clap and smile with elation. I see a bit of their big Brother Jesus in each of them.

I have sought to learn from my experience as a brother and from what the Bible teaches in order to better understand what it means when Jesus says he is not ashamed to call me his brother. When we are adopted into God's family, we became his children, and God becomes our Father. My siblings and I have the same parents and the same blood in a sense, the same gene pool from which to draw. A connection exists that no other human can claim, and because of that, we have a special relationship that binds us together. In a similar way, we are bound together with Jesus by his blood and by his Father.

Let's look at what Jesus did to bring about this relationship. My source for believing that Jesus is not ashamed to call us "brothers and sisters" is found in Hebrews 2:5-18. It all started when Jesus became a human with flesh and blood so that he could be like his brothers in every way. He even suffered death for the purpose of destroying death and the evil one in order to make us holy. That is the central message from God in all Scripture; it's the gospel. Because of the sacrificial work of Jesus, he says this powerful and astounding proclamation, "I am not ashamed to call them brothers and sisters (v. 11)." Hear this deeply: Jesus, the God-man, is calling those who put all their trust in him, brothers and sisters! He is not only unashamed, he also is proud to have us in his family. He is even proud to declare your name as a brother or sister in the presence of the congregation because we are one of the children God has given Jesus. That ought to send excitement to your heart and mind. Why can he do this? There is a family connection that brings mankind into this unique relationship with Jesus. We are connected by his blood and have the same parent, the Father God Almighty!

Brotherhood brings benefits and blessings in this family of God connection. Jesus is the pacesetter in dealing with temptation and life issues. Because Jesus suffered in his work of atonement and because he can sympathize with us as he was tempted in every way, we can approach the throne of grace with confidence to receive mercy and grace when in need (2:14-18, 4:15-16). This is our big Brother's providing and protecting us not only from death and the devil, but also from temptation by his grace and mercy. That is what big Brothers do.

It is important to note that Jesus calls us brothers, but there is no scriptural reference to believers calling him Brother. I don't quite understand this and don't need to. Mainly, I need to see him as my Savior and Lord without having to refer to him as "my brother." It could be that he is the one who is always in the role as big brother, who sets the pace for life and holiness and as the protector of little brother and sister. Jesus's work was meant to conform us into the likeness of God's Son so that Jesus would be the firstborn among many brothers (Romans 8:29). He is preeminent in the family of brothers, and we will spend eternity worshipping and praising Jesus our Lord and Savior.

The Bridegroom-bride Relationship

As I write about this beautiful relationship, it just hit me that today is my anniversary. How blessed I have been to have a special wife sent by God.

You may remember, one of my mentors encouraged me to begin praying for my future wife, and I think that was the first thing I began to pray for on a regular basis. If fact, I prayed for seven years. It all started one summer when I recruited a busload of high school students from Knoxville, Tennessee, to go with me to a Young Life Camp outside Buena Vista, Colorado. I was in a counselors' meeting when I met this pretty girl from Deerfield, Illinois, named Linda Harmon. We talked shop and that was it, it except for a few encounters during the week as we did activities such as snow sliding and horseback riding with the campers.

Interestingly, two girls who worked with me as volunteers in the Young Life club in Knoxville had come out to camp with me on the bus. They suggested I pursue this good-looking godly girl from Illinois. I was too focused on my camper-guys to have time for anything else. However, Linda decided to send me a letter of encouragement by way of these two girls. I received it and was very encouraged as she affirmed me on my dedication to my guys, desiring that they begin a relationship with Jesus. Linda would say that she didn't write her return address but wanted me to take the first step to pursue her. I jokingly say, she did include her phone number and ten dollars.

I did invite her to come to Knoxville for a visit and we got together for about five weekend visits. The summer after we met I decided to move to her hometown to really get to know her because we had really mainly dated by mail, phone, and a few visits. After a week I knew I wanted to marry her, but I didn't want to make a quick decision, as this was super important. So I waited one more week before asking her to marry me. We married seven weeks later; almost a year to date from when we first met, and seven years since I had started praying for my future wife.

Marriage is truly designed by God and the oneness relationship is the greatest relationship a human can experience. That oneness involves the total person: spiritual, physical, and mental. It also includes dreaming together, going through joys and pains together, and growing old together. I have sought to be the lover and leader God has called me to be, and she has stood with me and respected me through the process. We have had struggles with money, communication, sickness, and children dealing with life issues, failures, and successes. Being one with each other and with God has made our marriage what God designed it to be.

Jesus says that his marriage with us as believers or the church is very much like human marriages. He is our Bridegroom and we are his bride.

For most men I know, including me, this next relationship is not the one I want to think about because as a man I don't readily identify with the bridegroom and bride motif. My wife definitely does more than I do, as I'm sure many women do. Unfortunately, many men and women have deep, gashing wounds from experiencing a divorce in which the bride and/or bridegroom failed miserably. I don't minimize this pain, as I have counseled many couples who carry devastating wounds.

I believe that Jesus can meet you at the point of your needs and disappointments and through them teach you in a richer manner than those with good marriages because you are looking to be in the type of relationship I will describe from the biblical revelation. Let your pain and hunger take you deeper in understanding and longing to experience what God has.

The Song of Solomon is a beautiful picture of a husband and a wife expressing their love and intimacy to one another. Many in the Jewish tradition and Christian scholars see this Old Testament book as a picture of the deep relationship that God has with his people, with him being the Bridegroom and believers being the bride. In the Song of Solomon 1:15-16, the bridegrooms says, "How beautiful you are, my darling! Oh, how beautiful!" And she responds, "How handsome you are, my beloved! Oh, how charming!" John the Baptist gave testimony to the forthcoming Messiah by saying he was not the Christ but was sent ahead of him to prepare the way for him (John 3:27). John, as a friend of Jesus who "waits and listens for him," sees himself (and we join him as believers) as "the bride who belongs to the bridegroom."

As a result of being in a love relationship, being betrothed to Jesus, John experiences joy that is now complete. We experience that same complete joy when we are "in Jesus," who is our Bridegroom and we his bride. Grasp the ramifications of being betrothed to Jesus. Don't settle for just showing up at a wedding ceremony, walking the aisle, or praying a quick sinner's prayer, but love the One who loves you. Celebrate with great joy and dancing over this intimate love relationship. Jesus said that his friends, guests, and children should not fast or mourn when he, the Bridegroom, is in their presence (Mark 2:19-20).

In writing Ephesians 5:21-33, the apostle Paul is definitely speaking of a marriage between a man and a woman, but the essence and foundation of his argument are based on the "marriage" between Jesus and the church of believers. There is a holy union or betrothal between Jesus and believers that is expressed as a oneness, which is what we have been looking at in Jesus's teachings in John 14-17. Paul says this oneness is a profound mystery that exists between "Christ and the church." We are his bride and enjoy all the benefits of being in that love relationship. In this marriage-oneness with Jesus, Paul points out the mighty, essential work and sacrifice that Jesus encountered so that we would be his bride. Jesus "gave himself up" for the church (Ephesians 5:25). When he came and dwelled among us in bodily form and endured the pain and suffering on the cross, paying for our sins so that we could be in personal relationship with God, it was the ultimate sacrifice. He gave up his life to bring about forgiveness. In Romans 5:6, Paul says, "At just the right time, when we were still powerless, Christ died for the ungodly." A few verses later, Paul writes, "But he demonstrates his own love for us in this: While we were still sinners, Christ died for us (v. 8)." Thus, the marriage with Jesus began, but it didn't stop there.

There is so much more that Jesus does in this love relationship. Paul continues to show how the marriage we have with our Bridegroom is expressed in the following: first, he leads the church, his bride. As the leader, he is the head (Ephesians 5:23). He is in control and the Lord of this marriage love relationship. I can't think of a better one to be our leader because he has our best interests in mind. Yes, the One who laid down his life for us wants to lead us in a way that blesses and benefits us. Jesus's headship is based on his being the Savior (v. 23). Because of his role as Bridegroom, Leader, Head, and Savior, Jesus "feeds and cares for" (v. 29) his body (or bride). This means he is aware of our needs to be fed, nourished, and protected. His care for our lives isn't just for the temporal needs, but he desires to transform us into his image so that he can present us to himself as a bride that is radiant, without stain or wrinkle or any blemish, but holy and blameless (v. 29).

We are all familiar with the fairytale about Cinderella. The prince invited her and her two stepsisters to the ball, but Cinderella was unable to go until the fairy godmother showed up. As you know, Cinderella attended the ball, was beautiful, and the prince fell in love with her. In order to meet the midnight deadline, however, she had to rush out, losing her glass slipper along the way. Back home the ugly sisters abused her until one day the prince, going house to house, came looking for the young woman on whose foot the slipper would fit, so that he could redeem her and present her to himself as the radiant bride without blemish. This is exactly what Jesus is doing for us, his bride. He gave up his life for us and is now in the process of making us whole, beautiful, perfect, and glorious. Look at what John saw and heard in Revelation 21:1-4:

> **Then I saw a new heaven and a new earth, for the first heaven and the first earth had passed away, and there was no longer any sea. I saw the Holy City, the New Jerusalem, coming down out of heaven from God, prepared as a bride beautifully dressed for her husband. And I heard a loud voice from the throne saying, "Look! God's dwelling place is now among the people, and he will dwell with them. They will be his people, and God himself will be with them and be their God. He will wipe every tear from their eyes. There will be no more death or mourning or crying or pain, for the old order of things has passed away."**

Here we see the "bride beautifully dressed for her husband" because Jesus has completed the work of restoration and newness and completeness. Look at this love marriage relationship that is planned for the bride, the dwelling of God is "with men" and he will live "with them." They will be his people and God himself will be "with them" and be their God. What a relationship! It doesn't get any better than this.

It is intriguing that God would use the metaphors of reality to communicate the relationship we as believers have with him. They are truly the inner circle of our most meaningful in-depth relationships that humans can have.

My wife has taught me more about God than anyone. She has loved me unconditionally even in the good, bad, and ugly. I mentioned that I read on a sixth-grade level when I finished high school and hated reading out loud. I remember practicing reading in front of Linda, knowing she loved me and wouldn't be critical of me. She has stuck with me with my wild ideas and desire for adventure, and even when I have led us to places of uncertainty. She is a flesh-picture of always being there. In her wedding vows she quoted from the book of Ruth, "Your people will be my people and your God my God. (Ruth 1:16)."

As I write this, it is likely some of you have not had these types of relationships for various reasons, but that should not hinder you from what God has for you. Scripture says that he is the Husband of the widow and the Father of the fatherless. In Christ we have all the benefits, no matter what our earthly relationship is. As humans we don't have the capacity to have too many in-depth relationships, but the relationships we have with our father (and, of course, our mother), our siblings, our few close friends, and our spouse are the most powerful and meaningful. This is ideal but not always experienced on the human level.

God has brought all of them together in our relationship with him. As Father, he oversees and guides us through the big picture by coaching and disciplining us. As Brother, Jesus has that family connection with us and he cares for and helps us live up to the family name. I believe he is proud of us and pleased to call us brother. As Friend, Jesus has our front, sides, and back, and he stands with us with no agenda and no role to fulfill, just be our friend or cohort. As Bridegroom, Jesus is the one who loves us with a love that is even greater than the love Hosea had for his adulterous prostitute wife, Gomer. He is our provider and protector who continues to lay his life down for us and pray for us.

❧

Group discussion questions:

Hook:

a. Talk about what it means to you to be in a Father-son or Father-daughter relationship with the Creator.

b. Talk about what it means to you to be in a Brother-brother or Brother-sister relationship with Jesus.

c. Talk about what it means to be in a Friend-friend relationship with Jesus.

d. Would a few couples in the group take a few minutes and tell how you met your spouses? If appropriate, share how the marriage has been a gift from God.

1. Head. Discuss how incredible it is to be able to call God "Abba." Talk about what it means to the church for Jesus to lay his life down for his bride.

2. Heart. Each should try to get in touch with what you feel, thinking of Jesus laying his life down for you. How does that thought impact you on a regular basis?

3. Head. We understand that as Christ's bride we are called to submit to our Bridegroom. How does having a loving leader affect our submission to him?

4. Heart. Now that you have thought about this Bridegroom-bride relationship, how does it really excite you and communicate with you the significance of this relationship God invited us into? Where are you still having trouble with it?

5. Hand. Take some time as a group and pray about these four relationships and the different ramifications for oneness with God.

9

Oneness with the Holy Spirit

"You are the Christ, the Son of the living God."
— Peter, one of Jesus's disciples
MATTHEW 16:16
⤳

T HIS IS AN ESPECIALLY IMPORTANT CHAPTER FOR THOSE OF YOU
WHO are seeking to live this personal relationship with Jesus.
I sense most Christians are seeking to live the Christian life
in their own strength. This will be great practical news for you.

If we know we are "in Christ" (a son or daughter of his), we can
begin to live out who we are. But guess what? We don't have the ability on our own to do this, because of our sin nature, our weaknesses,
our bad motives, and our self-centeredness and just plain independent stance. Living a life that is God-honoring and comes from the
inside out must have the power of the Holy Spirit within.

A verse that sums up this truth is found in Galatians 2:20, "I have
been crucified with Christ and I no longer live, but Christ lives in
me. The life I now live in the body, I live by faith in the Son of God,
who loved me and gave himself for me." There are two lives mentioned here: the life before being crucified with Christ, and the new
believer who lives by faith in the Son of God. The old life died with
Jesus, and the new believer lives with Jesus by the power of the Spirit.

The tendency is to try to live this "Christian life" by ourselves
and in our own strength. We say, "I can do it." Much of life is spent
by working hard and persevering so that we please our parents, by

99

performing for our teachers and coaches, and by being diligent workers in the marketplace. In trying to be a good Christian, it translates into self-effort, resulting in falling short of our desires to be good and godly. The "oughta, shoulda, coulda" defeats us. We can't be strong-willed enough.

Another response is that we try to appear more spiritual than we are. So often we look the part or speak the "God-talk," going through the right Christian activities in order to make others think we are really walking with God. There is no joy in living the life by our own strengths because we are out of relationship and not abiding with and in Jesus.

This vicious circle of trying to live the Christian life will wear us out. It is time to surrender to God by acknowledging that we can't do it this way.

I like the way Paul tells about how in his weakness, he needed help: "But he said to me, 'My grace is sufficient for you, for my power is made perfect in weakness.' Therefore I will boast all the more gladly about my weaknesses, so that Christ's power may rest on me. That is why, for Christ's sake, I delight in weaknesses, in insults, in hardships, in persecutions, in difficulties. For when I am weak, then I am strong." (2 Corinthians 12:9-10) This is a paradox in which my weaknesses are considered good because they cause me to call on the Holy Spirit. Remember, we are seeking a love relationship in which we are dependent on Jesus.

Let's look at what Jesus said about himself in John 12:23-24. Jesus replied, "The hour has come for the Son of Man to be glorified. Very truly I tell you, unless a kernel of wheat falls to the ground and dies, it remains only a single seed. But if it dies, it produces many seeds." He was referring to the fact that he was going to die on the cross, rise, and be glorified. Out of that mighty work, great things would be accomplished, mainly bringing believers into a saving relationship with God. A single seed will stay a single seed until it dies by going in the ground, germinating, growing, and producing many seeds. Likewise, we must die. If we don't die, Jesus says, "Anyone who loves their life will lose it, while anyone who hates their life in this world will keep it for eternal life." (John 12:25) As we learn to

100

"hate" this life, we become ready to die. Jesus said, "Apart from me you can do nothing." When we love this world and ourselves, we will not die, and as a result, we will produce nothing. Do you see the connection between becoming weak and dying? There is great benefit. Jesus, through the Holy Spirit, is available to give us strength and power, which is far beyond what we typically imagine. A physician from England, Hudson Taylor, who was a missionary to China for over fifty years in the last half of the 1800s, called the exchange of our weak lives for a Christ-living powerful life within us "the exchanged life." I think the phrase "the exchanged life" truly captures the essence of living in Christ's power.

One of the hardest things any of us has to do is to admit we are weak and can't live the life God is calling us to live. Only at that point of surrender when we are ready to do his work, are we empowered by his Spirit. The Bible basically says that works done by a believer would be like silver, gold, and precious stones that will withstand the test of fire at the final judgment (1 Corinthians 3:12). Works done just by human effort would burn up like wood, hay, or straw. Be careful that you do not make the mistake of saying that you will first do your best, and only when you become exhausted or fail will you then call on the Spirit. No, even in our strengths, we are helpless and need him. When we admit our weakness and helplessness and the Spirit empowers us, we live victoriously. This is what I refer to as the "exchanged life." I exchange my weak life for his. That leads to victory.

So, what is victory or success? Many preachers or evangelists appear on TV to proclaim the prosperity gospel, which can be confusing. Success is not measured by the world's standards but is tied to our relationship with God. It is in Christ. It is peace and joy, but it is also such a sense of contentment and faith in God that when we trust him inwardly, we sense all is well. Victory is faith. Success is faith in God and his will for us. As Jesus said in the garden before his crucifixion, "It is not my will but yours." I trust you, Father. "Now faith is confidence in what we hope for and assurance about what we do not see." (Hebrews 11:1) This doesn't mean life will be trouble-free; in fact, expect bumpy roads, hard times, doubts, lack of patience, and disappointment as you seek to live this life of trust in God. He is responsible for the outcome.

All of this is about a relationship with our Father and Jesus and the indwelling of the Holy Spirit. This personal relationship is all connected to the oneness with Jesus, the Vine, and living as a son or daughter of God.

Practically Living in the Power of the Holy Spirit

How does this living the exchanged life by the power of the Spirit work out in a practical sense? I will break down this experience into eight components so that I can explain the process; in actuality, though, you probably will not take these steps in order. However, there is value in thinking through the isolated parts of the process until it becomes more natural.

Truth No. 1: Know the Truth: Jesus and the Word of God, the Foundation

We have talked about this earlier, but I want to put the process of living in relationship with the Holy Spirit in those same terms. Jesus, in John 17:17, said in his prayer to his Father, "Your Word is truth." In John 14:6, Jesus said, "I am the truth," and in John 8:32 he said, "You will know the truth, and the truth will set you free." Every human being needs to base his or her life on truth in some form, whether it is scientific truth or legal truth, but specifically it needs to be truth revealed in the Person of Jesus and in the revealed Word of God. If we want to know Jesus, our relationship with him should be based on what has been revealed about him in both facts and understanding. We also need to know Jesus in a personal way.

The Bible is the foundation. We must seek to know the Word or Truth; we need to understand it and comprehend it. That is the

FOUNDATION:
TRUTH

reason we should read the Word, study it, pray about it, talk about it with others, and meditate on it. Our whole life philosophy or worldview is to be set on Truth, both the Word and Jesus. David said in Psalm 19:7-11 (italics denote author's emphasis):

> The law of the LORD is *perfect*, refreshing the soul. The statutes of the LORD are *trustworthy*, making wise the simple. The precepts of the LORD are *right*, giving joy to the heart. The commands of the LORD are *radiant*, giving light to the eyes. The fear of the LORD is *pure*, enduring forever. The *decrees* of the LORD are firm, and all of them are *righteous*. They are *more precious than gold*, than much pure gold; they are *sweeter* than *honey*, than honey from the honeycomb. By them your servant is *warned*; in keeping them there is *great reward*.

The Word is basically saying that it will address all areas of life. It is relevant, practical, and effective. We can base our life on it. It is right from the heart of God. Truth is truth if all believe it or no one believes it. It is not my truth but *the* Truth.

The big question here: Do you base everything on the Truth in Scripture and Jesus?

Truth No. 2: Believe the Truth, the Head

I have seen too many people who believe that the Bible is God's Word only in theory. They have participated in Bible studies and devotions, been a part of their local church, and said they believed all the right things until the Bible was contradictory to their lifestyle or what they wanted to do. I must confess I have been there, and if you examined my life even now, you and I would both conclude I am still there in too many areas. However, my desire is not to live my life in contradiction to God's Word. I find that those of us who live in a manner contrary to the Word are in denial in some areas, disobedient, or living merely as cultural Christians. I find the thing that causes me to want to live by Scripture is based on if I truly believe God's Word and love him enough to follow it. The combination of knowing that God did reveal his mind and then believing it equips me to follow what it says.

The big question here: Do I really believe that the Truth is true and from God?

This is a non-negotiable truth.

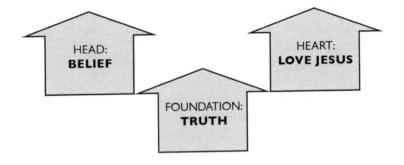

Truth No. 3: Love Jesus, the Heart

Belief in the truth is essential, but many times it isn't enough to motivate us to act on the truth. When belief and love for Jesus operate in tandem, things happen. We are ready to trust what God is saying in order to step out and do something about it. Loving Jesus with all our hearts, minds, and strength is the thing that moves us to action. We usually do what we love. We respond to people we love. God's main motivation for reaching out to us for a relationship was his deep love for us. We love him back by doing what he calls us to do. Love wins out. Belief in the truth and love for Jesus go together as great motivators for action.

The big question here: Do I *love* God enough to respond to his revealed truth with obedience? (Love is the motivation for obedience.)

To illustrate, the Bible says, "Thou shall not steal." So we ask ourselves this series of questions that engage your head, your heart, and your will:

- Do I believe that this truth is from God's mind and heart?
- Do I believe it is true?
- Do I love Jesus in a manner to the extent that I will seek to take action on this command?

Truth No. 4: Obey Jesus, the Will

We will discuss the power to do it later, but for now there are two points that need to be acknowledged: I believe the God-revealed biblical truth and I love Jesus. In response to my belief in the Bible and deep love and affection for Jesus, will I seek to obey it? We have a choice: yes or no. I find this combination gives me all I need to step out in faith and obey. If I don't have a high view of the authority of Scripture, if I just

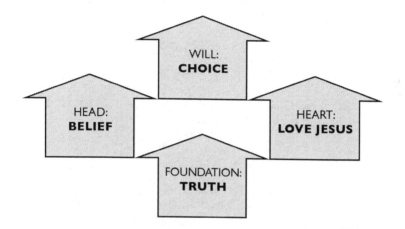

give it lip service, or I really don't have a love for Jesus, I will disobey many times. Sometimes I will obey, but that could be that I am just acting for selfish gain, doing the right thing for the wrong reasons.

Assuming our motives are correct, now we are ready to seek to obey the Truth. The big question here: Do I *choose* to obey the Truth?

Truth No. 5: Invite the Holy Spirit to Empower You

Now is when the Holy Spirit must be invited in. He is just one prayer or one ask away. We desire to obey the truth by choosing to obey it. Now we need the Spirit to empower us; so we invite him in, and then obey. How does that happen? I don't know, but it does happen. Where do my choosing and the Spirit come in to empower me? I don't know, but it happens. All we can do is trust him.

Frankly, I don't know when my effort ends and his begins. All I

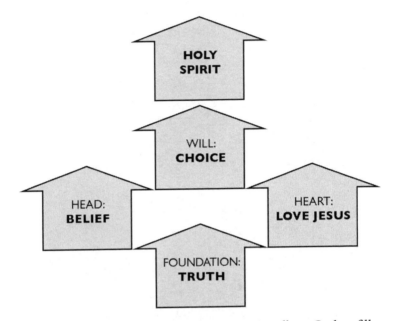

know is it happens. The Spirit shows up. We call on God to fill us with his Spirit so that we will be empowered to do what he has asked us to do. This goes back to the relationship between a child of God (you and me) and God himself. It is a relationship of love and power.

The big question here: Do I realize that even in my strengths, I am weak? I am helpless. I need to ask the Holy Spirit to give me understanding and power to obey.

Jesus said that when we are weak, we call on him to give us the grace and power to do what he says. This is the relationship he is looking for: a dependent walk of faith. This leads to the next truth.

Truth No. 6: Trust Jesus to Work in Me: The Step of Faith

Let me assure you, it is not easy stepping out in faith to do what he asks. In fact, you might do exactly what he wants yet things still will not work out for you the way you had hoped or believed they would. God has his timing and his ways, so he will take care of the results. Trust him. In Hebrews 11:6, the author sums this up well, "It is impossible to please God apart from faith." Paul confirms this when

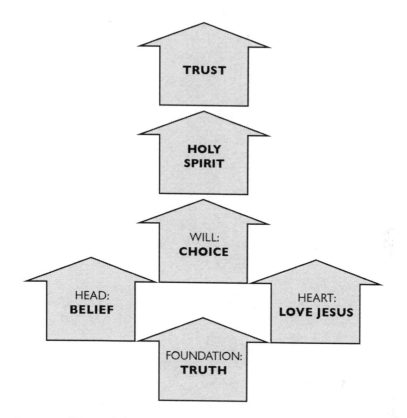

he writes, "Everything that does not come from faith is sin." Obeying is an act of faith. The big question here: Do I *trust* God to work through me in my weaknesses and strengths as I choose to obey with the power of the Holy Spirit?

Truth No. 7: Expect Struggles as You Step Out with Trust: The Potential Frustration

Make it a point to acknowledge your frustration and disappointment when things don't work the way you anticipated. Tell him your struggles because you are in a love relationship; you have the freedom to share your heart with him. He wants you to express yourself. Leave the results to him. This will lead to what I call success or victory from our perspective and God's. From our side we have relied on the Word

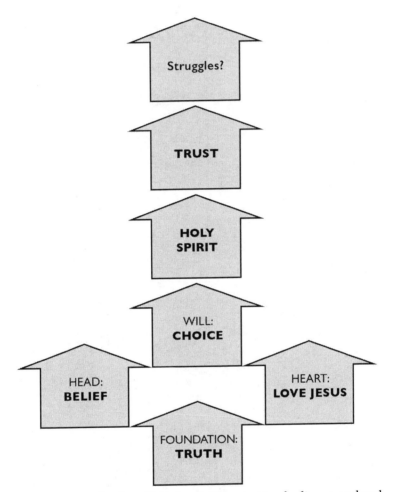

of God, believed it, loved him by stepping out in obedience, and realized we can't live the Christian life in our own strength, so we call on his Spirit to give us the power to live. As we go through the struggling process, we trust him no matter what the results are, because we know he is in control. It is exchanging our weakness for his strength.

The big question here: Do I realize there might be *struggles* in this trusting process? These might include disappointments, failure, attacks, and times of "I don't understand why God doesn't answer as I want him to."

There was a time in my life when my wife and I got sideways with another couple. We had been in each other's homes as our children played together; we had been out to dinner together; we had even vacationed together for a weekend in another state. We had dreamed and prayed about bringing our families up together in the ways of the Lord. All of a sudden, this other couple began to close us off and act coldly toward us. This not only hurt, it also was confusing. We wanted a right relationship with our friends, and so Linda and I looked to see what the Bible had to say. We thought of the verses in Joshua 1:8: "Keep this Book of the Law always on your lips; meditate on it day and night, so that you may be careful to do everything written in it. Then you will be prosperous and successful." Also Jesus said, "Therefore, if you are offering your gift at the altar and there remember that your brother or sister has something against you, leave your gift there in front of the altar. First go and be reconciled to them; then come and offer your gift" (Matthew 5:23-24). To obey the Bible meant we had to humble ourselves and go to them to be reconciled. That was awkward! We didn't want to do it. They had cut us off for no apparent reason.

We didn't have a peace from God to just let it go, move on, and find other friends. After asking the Holy Spirit to empower us, we went to them, taking it upon ourselves to shoulder much of the blame for our relationship being out of balance, and in so doing asked them if we could reconcile. In some ways it felt right as we talked with them, but in the weeks to come nothing seemed to change. Confused even more, we wrote them a letter and then visited them again.

At some point in all this, I didn't feel like it was right to take the Lord's Supper at church because things just weren't right. It turned out that the husband in this other couple didn't feel right taking it either. Right after the church service where we had tried to take communion, he and I went to our pastor telling him what we felt. At that time there was confession and reconciliation, only to see still no change in the weeks to come. How devastating and unbiblical. Linda and I struggled, continuing to wonder what we had done and why we couldn't reconcile. We were open to not being best friends, but not open to being unreconciled.

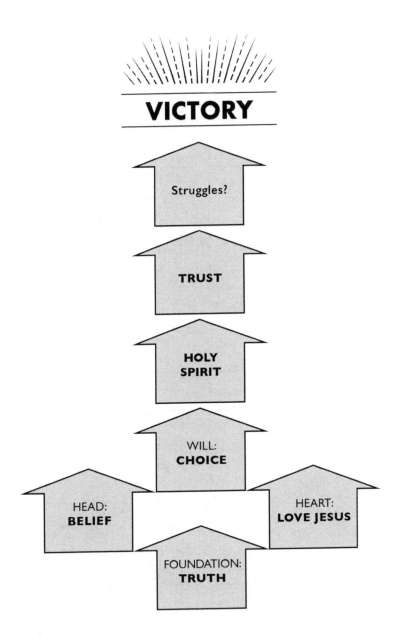

Finally, I called the husband and with an intense tone to my voice and probably plenty of anger, I said, "The Kingdom of God doesn't exist in our relationship, and God is not glorified. We have come to you trying to reconcile and have trusted God to bring us together. I am not coming anymore. The ball is in your park." I have not seen or talked to them since. I don't know what state they live in, but if they were to call today and say we could reconcile, I would say, "Stay right there, I will come to you."

Now the rest of the story: I have complete peace and victory or even success before God. Why? I chose to obey the Bible. I asked the Holy Spirit to fill me, and I trust him for the results. Sadly, we remain unreconciled as I write this. Is that success or victory? No, it is not victory in the sense of being reconciled, but yes, it is success in the sense of doing all I knew to do while trusting the remainder to God.

Truth No. 8: There Is Victory and Success Waiting for Us: The Goal

We will probably find many situations where we obey God's word, but the results we are looking for don't show up. For example, praying for a job, praying for healing of a family member, or giving out of obedience but not seeing the outcome we were hoping for. God is still in control and he will work things out according to his purposes (Romans 8:28). We can count on him. He is trustworthy, loving, all-powerful, and sovereign over all. He has our best interests in mind. Success or victory is manifested in just our trusting him. Leave the results to him. The big question: Do I desire to *thank* and *trust* God for the results, whether they are positive or negative? *Trusting is victory!*

One way to picture this relationship is with a gardener and his glove. A gardener goes to plant his field in order to produce a crop. Of course, he needs gloves to protect his hands while breaking up the soil, hoeing, planting the seed, fertilizing, watering the plants, and picking weeds out of the garden. So the gardener tells the glove to get to work and do what it was designed to do. Of course the glove just lies there on the table and absolutely nothing happens in terms of tending the garden. So the gardener challenges more and seeks to motivate the glove, but all to no avail. Finally, the gardener realizes he must put his own hand in the glove for it to function properly. That is a picture of each of us realizing that we can't do what we want to do spiritually in our own strength. We need the Holy Spirit. Paul writes the Corinthians to tell them "we have this treasure (the Holy Spirit) in jars of clay (our bodies, minds, strengths, experience) to show that this all-surpassing power is from God and not from us." (2 Corinthians 4:7)

> *Lord Jesus, when I think that I am a "jar of clay," that can be a downer for me. It takes me back to the old self where I saw myself as a failure and feared failure. Help me see myself the way you see me—as a son or daughter of yours, yet still clay that is powerless to do Kingdom or spiritual things on my own. Fill me with your Spirit!*

The following is a summary of the exchanged life chart. Start with No. 1 (The Foundation) and work your way up to No. 8 (The Victory).

8. **THE VICTORY!** Do I desire to THANK and TRUST God for the results whether they are positive or negative? TRUSTING is VICTORY!

7. **THE STRUGGLES:** Do I realize there will be STRUGGLES in this trusting process? These may include disappointments, feelings of failure, attacks, frustrations, and times I don't understand why God doesn't answer as I want Him to.

6. **THE TRUST:** Do I TRUST God to work through me in my weaknesses and strengths as I choose to obey with the power of the Holy Spirit?

5. **THE HOLY SPIRIT:** Do I realize that even in my strengths, I am weak? I need to ask the HOLY SPIRIT to give me understanding and the power to obey.

4. **THE WILL:** Do I CHOOSE to obey the truth?

3. **THE HEART:** Do I LOVE God enough to respond to his revealed truth with obedience? (Love is a motivation for obedience.)

2. **THE HEAD:** Do I really BELIEVE that the truth is true and from God? (Belief is a motivation for obedience.)

1. **THE FOUNDATION:** Do I base everything on the TRUTH from Scripture?

Group Discussion Questions:

Hook: Talk about a time when you felt the Holy Spirit empowering you do to something God wanted you to do. You knew the results didn't come from you, but you stepped out in obedience.

1. Head. Consider these two statements: "The Bible is my truth" and, "The Bible is the Truth." How are these different, and how would the difference affect how we live? How do we respond to God's commands?

2. Head. As a group, talk about how the combination of our belief in the truth of the Bible and our love for Jesus must go hand in hand when it comes to obeying God's Word. Can you think of a situation in which you or a friend disobeyed the Bible, yet claimed to believe the direction was from God?

3. Heart. Talk about how natural it is to try to do religious activity, or to perform in our own strength to obey God's Word.

4. Heart. Talk about how unnatural it is to admit our weaknesses or to ask for help from anyone, as well as from God. How do you feel when you do this? How is weakness the beginning of strength? (See 2 Corinthians 12:9-10.)

5. Hand. Explain how and why the human will is essential in obedience. How do the Holy Spirit and the human will work together? When does the human will end and God's Spirit step in?

6. Hand. Victory is trusting God for the outcome. How is trust an action on our part? What does it look like in very tough situations? How do trust, struggles, and victory cause us to have a multitude of feelings, both positive and negative?

Part III

A Oneness with Our Friends

10

Friends Standing Together

"I know you are the holy one of Israel."
— A man possessed by an impure spirit
MARK 1:24
⌖

"Church isn't what it should be."

"I feel like I am just going through the motions."

"I think I will just stay home and meet with the Lord on my own or watch a sermon on TV."

"I don't have any connections or friends at church."

IN MY UNDERSTANDING, TWENTY-THREE MILLION CHRISTIANS WHO HAVE checked out of church with similar comments, are called "nones" since they have no church. They are missing out on corporate worship and potential fellowship. Many millennials have completely abandoned church as well.

In church circles there has been talk about desiring to have a New Testament church where believers live in an ideal relationship with each other, worshiping God regularly and praying without ceasing. That sounds very noble and spiritual, except there's a problem with that premise—there is ambiguity in defining what a New Testament church is so that everyone can agree on it.

Still, let's give it a shot. Maybe we're talking about the New Testament church that dates back to right after Jesus ascended. Or it could be the Corinthian church that was rife with a lot of strife and ungodliness. The latter sounds like an embarrassment, but it probably more closely describes what we are experiencing today, where churches are dealing with real-life issues.

Collectively, we have an unrealistic view of what our church experience should be, based on how the church operates today. It is pretty much impossible to experience real in-depth fellowship as recorded in the New Testament. Many churches today focus only on the worship service between eleven and twelve on Sunday morning, along with activities at the corner of Third and Broadway or any church address where churchgoers attend. Some churches have the feel of a theater in which members flock in as spectators to see the next performance. When it is over, they file out the doors, soon to be replaced by another group of spectators coming in right behind the first group. I believe God is calling us to a spiritual experience better than any of this.

In this chapter I am going to emphasize mainly the small group aspect of the church where people have a chance to connect with others. Please continue your corporate worship in a church that has the best combination for you with teaching, singing, and worship in general.

I'm not picking on any particular church, or even any one denomination under the Christian umbrella. The theatrical flavor of churches is actually pretty common. There is great value in corporate worship. But I can remember only a few times where I have experienced "church" that had the look and feel of what God had in mind for the church. One such time involved a group of twelve men, two of them black, and I was the oldest man there—probably old enough to be the same age as many of their fathers. But we really connected.

In our little group we discovered plenty of common interests, ranging from basketball to which type of service projects we enjoyed. Some of us drove to the border waters of the USA and Canada to grow our beards, fish, canoe, and break wind together. We even bought several season tickets for the Tennessee Titans professional football games and shared them, taking turns going in smaller groups. Probably the most connecting times were when we dealt with life issues such as money, marriage, kids, health, and work.

We had free "consulting" sessions among ourselves, dug into Scripture to see what God had to say about certain things, and shouldered one another's problems before the Lord in prayer. The thing that drew us together the most over those two years was when one brother faced some very tough marriage issues. We could only stand with him and hurt and pray for him, hoping things would turn out differently. In all the pain and fun we had sharing life together, it had that Kingdom-come-on-earth feel. We even buried one of our brothers a few years after the group ended. We cared, confronted, loved, and opened up our hearts and minds. We were truly a band of brothers.

Another time I experienced church as I believe God intended it occurred at my church where I am a member. We had a pastor who preached truth from the Bible, and every sentence he spoke was packed. I remember running off a hard copy of many sermons, and I would meditate on the content in the days that followed. The highlight, for me, was the Sunday school class that followed the service and was led by a couple. The sermon was challenging, but the discussion was even more intense. We unpacked the truth presented by our pastor and took it to the grass-roots level. Individuals felt free to speak openly and to seek the truth together. Unfortunately, it was only one hour out of the week and didn't go far enough. That class had some qualities that I have to believe were very similar to what early believers experienced.

Jesus prayed that we would experience a fellowship centered on him that would incorporate the greatest commands of loving God and loving one another. It is what we are longing for in our church life.

In the New Testament there are more than thirty references calling believers to interact with one another in order to live out this dynamic oneness that Jesus prayed for in John 17. Calling them "The One Another Circle," I have summarized these into six that seem to summarize the thirty:

a. **Encourage one another:** Hebrews 3:13, I Thessalonians 5:11; don't grumble with one another, James 5:9; build up one another, I Thessalonians 5:11; offer hospitality to one another, I Peter 4:9; greet one another with a holy kiss, Romans 16:16

b. **Forgive one another:** Colossians 3:13. bear with one another, Ephesians 4:2; don't judge one another, Romans 14:13; accept one another, Romans 15:17; confess sins to one another, James 5:16; stop passing judgment on one another, Romans 14:13

c. **Submit to one another:** Ephesians 5:21; be patient with one another, Ephesians 4:2; accept one another, Romans 15:7; be devoted to one another, Romans 12:10; be at peace with one another, Mark 9:50

d. **Admonish one another:** Colossians 3:16; instruct one another, Romans 15:14; spur on to love and good deeds, Hebrews 10:24-25

e. **Honor one another:** Romans 12:10, I Peter 4:9; do not slander one another, James 4:11; pray for one another, James 5:16

f. **Love one another:** Romans 13:8, I John 3:11, Ephesians 3:23, 4:7, 11, 12, 32, John 13:34-35; be kind, compassionate, serve one another, Galatians 5:13; live in harmony with one another, Romans 12:16

The One Another Circle

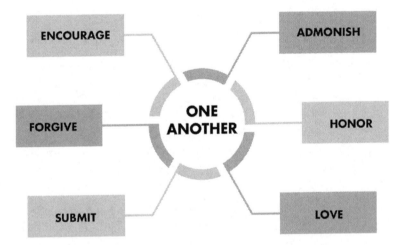

The Oneness Desired by Jesus for Believers

In John 17, Jesus prays for oneness among believers. This is also a mystery, similar but different from the oneness, depicted in John 14:20. Jesus said, "I am in my Father, and you are in me and I in you." The oneness that the Father has with Jesus, and which believers have with the Father and Son, is instructional; it also demonstrates the oneness that can exist in a group of believers. There is caring, communicating, and being on the same agenda. Likewise, the oneness and fellowship that are talked about in the Bible can exist in a small group and can be instructional to believers about their oneness with Jesus. Our fellowship groups need to consist of lots of loving one another, encouraging one another, and submitting to one another. It is in this oneness that believers can truly learn to experience the oneness they have with Jesus.

The discipleship process is lived out in fellowship. The Word of God, life issues, and followers of Jesus will intersect. The Spirit of God shows up to lead in truth, and to empower us and to transform lives. Believers experience love and forgiveness. They discover one another's gifts and point them out. They have fun, experience connectedness, and begin to think of going beyond themselves to always being there for others around them. Believers are meant to experience fellowship and oneness with one another. This is a picture of the human relational part of church. There are meeting needs, praying with one another, being real and vulnerable, and even challenging and confronting each other when needed. Believers were made for this type of fellowship.

There are four major points (I have written about the first three in chapters 4-7) on oneness described in John, chapters 14-17, that relate to abiding in Jesus. First, there's the oneness ("I in the Father and he in Me" 14:10-11) between the Father and the Son that is the foundation of the oneness that is available to us. Second, there's the oneness between believers with the Father and the Son ("I am in my Father and you in me and I in you" 14:20). The third is the oneness between the Holy Spirit and a believer (John 14:16-17). The fourth is the oneness between the body of believers with each other and which connects to the Divine Oneness (Jesus prayed "that they be one as we are one . . . so that they may be brought to complete unity." 17:22-23) I have dealt with the first three in earlier chapters, now I will deal with the fourth.

1. Oneness between Father-Son (F-S) John 14:11

2. Oneness between Father-Son-Believers (F-S-B) John 14:20

3. Oneness between Holy Spirit-Believer (S-B) John 14:16-17

4. Oneness between Believers (B-B) John 17:22

Jesus prays that the disciples would be sanctified: "Sanctify them by the truth; your word is truth." 17:17 Sanctify means to be set apart for a special use or purpose, and even a "set-apart" relationship. This set-apartness is for the purpose of being in a unique

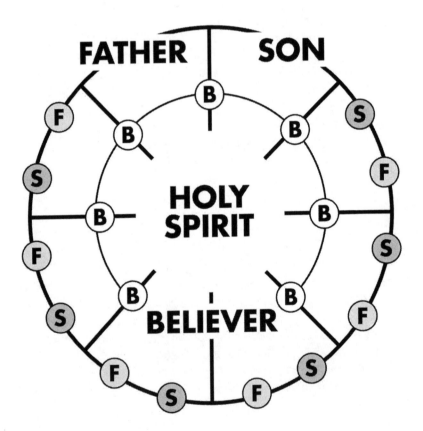

and special relationship with Jesus and with his followers. This relationship is in the Spiritual dimension with Jesus and between believers. This is what Jesus prays for. Look at the call for oneness (between the Trinity and believer) that Jesus prays from John 17:

- *they* may be **one as we are one** (v. 11)
- all of *them* may be **one**, Father, just as **you are in me and I am in you.** (v. 21a)
- May *they* also be **in us** (v. 21b)
- I have given *them* the glory that you gave me, that *they* **may be one as we are one** (v. 22)
- they may **be one as we are one** (v. 22)
- **I in** *them* **and you in me** (v. 23)
- so that *they* may be brought to **complete unity** (v. 23)
- love you have for me may be *in them* **and that I myself may be** *in them* (v. 26)
- that *they* too may be truly **sanctified** (set apart in this unique holy relationship of oneness) (v. 19)
- and the full measure of **joy within** *them* (v. 13)

This oneness is beyond comprehension but is a reality and must be taken by faith just because Jesus said it is true and real. It happens in our spiritual connectedness to the Trinity and, in some way, with believers as they are connected with each other in Jesus. The connection between the Father, Son, and Holy Spirit is different from the connectedness with believers. The Father and Son are "in" each other and we are "in" them but our siblings are not "in" each other. There is a family connection as a child of God but not a direct Spirit connection between siblings. The Spirit shows up " . . . when two or three are gathered in my name, I am with them" (Matthew 18.20). The Spirit is in each believer. The presence of the Spirit of God brings about the oneness on a spiritual level that carries over to believers when we are gathered and even when we are apart. That's because we are in the same family. We have a role in building that oneness with fellow believers by being proactive, which goes with a responsibility to build our relationship with God. We pursue him because he has pursued us. We are called to abide or remain in the Vine and we are called to be in oneness with each other.

We discussed earlier what it looks like to abide in Jesus—by knowing, loving, trusting, obeying, and praising him. In a similar manner, we are called to abide with each other and the body of believers, "That all of them may be one, Father, *just as* (emphasis mine) you are in me and I am in you." (John 17:21) I don't think it is the same oneness as between the Father and Son, but Jesus says, " . . . just as . . . ," so there are some similarities to oneness.

Each of the five pillars of abiding I wrote about in Chapter 6 applies to the oneness Jesus is praying for all of his disciples—those on earth with him and those who would come after him. Let's look at each individually (in the following comments I apply the ideas from Chapter 6 about how abiding refers to knowing, loving, trusting, obeying, and praising Jesus. We do a similar thing in bringing about the oneness with believers. I call these the five pillars of abiding):

a. As we seek to know everything Scripture reveals about Jesus, and as we seek to really *know* him personally in this love relationship, we seek to know our fellow believers by finding out about their lives, their history, their motivations, and their passions. We all have a built-in need to know and be known. For example, we love it when someone asks us about how we started our business or what excites us about work or how one of our children is doing at school. We want them to be vulnerable when we ask how they are doing or ask deep questions of them. Likewise we need to be honest with ourselves by revealing our thoughts, feelings, and dreams. Believers are (or at least should be) real with each other because we are in the same family and have the same Father. Having Jesus in common in the spiritual dimension frees us up to speak into our relationship with each other and to seek to know one another deeply.

b. Being in a *love* relationship with Jesus gives us a new identity and frees us up to move into a love relationship with one another. As we love Jesus, we love each other unconditionally, expressing love, admonishing, confronting, challenging, and encouraging, and through all that we come alongside one another. Just as we are designed to know and be known, we are designed after our Savior to love and be loved. "I have made you *known* to them, and will continue to make you known (emphasis mine) in order that the love you have for me may be in them and that I myself may be in them." (John 17:26) Knowing and loving go hand in hand. Knowing Jesus and loving Jesus are directly connected to knowing and loving one another. Look at three passages from 1 John 4:

- "Dear friends, let us love one another, for love comes from God. Everyone who loves has been born of God and knows God. Whoever does not love does not know God, because God is love." (1 John 4:7-8)

- "If anyone acknowledges that Jesus is the Son of God, God lives in them and they in God. And so we know and rely on the love God has for us. God is love. Whoever lives in love lives in God, and God in them." (1 John 4: 15-16)

- "We love because he first loved us. Whoever claims to love God yet hates a brother or sister is a liar. For whoever does not love their brother and sister, whom they have seen, cannot love God, whom they have not seen. And he has given us this command: Anyone who loves God must also love their brother and sister." (1 John 4: 19-21)

c. As we trust Jesus, we *trust* one another by believing in them, seeing potential, standing with them, investing in them, and sharing life and resources with them. "Trust" says to our fellow believers that we respect and value them just for who they are. It is tied to the friendship we have with one another. They can speak into our lives and we into theirs. The author of Hebrews says to confess your sins to one another and to pray for one another. It takes trust to confess. We only do it with those with whom we have a sanctified relationship. Again, learning to trust Jesus can lay the groundwork for trusting each other, especially as we center on the Word of God. Likewise, learning to trust one another can address trusting Jesus. Knowing one another can assist in helping us love others and trust them. They are all connected.

d. As we *obey* Jesus, we submit to one another by valuing, respecting, honoring, and even being accountable to others by allowing them to have authority over us when they have won the right to. Having authority over someone can easily be misused and always needs to be in line with the Scriptures. There are those to whom we are called to yield, such as parents, bosses, and church elders, as well as to one another. Ephesians 5:21 says to submit to one another.

e. When we see all that Jesus does and who he is, it is natural to *praise* him. I don't think we are called to praise one another the way we praise and glorify Jesus, but there is an appropriate form of praise or recognition. I like to honor or affirm others by acknowledging strengths, weaknesses, potential, and spiritual gifts. We see value as we hang out together and get to know each other. Out of love, we want to affirm them. We speak the truth in love because we are one. We call forth one another's gifts by seeing strengths and potential. Words have the power of life and death (Proverbs 18:21).

Living Out This Oneness or In-ness Practicality

I have sought to lay out the inexpressible spiritual dimension of oneness between the Father and Son so that a believer can join that oneness or "in-ness." It is a union that is reality, but at the same time, a mystery. After Jesus ascended into heaven following his resurrection, the disciples and a few women went to Jerusalem and into the Upper Room to pray in one accord (Acts 1:14)

I am going to introduce a Greek word that captures the essence of fellowship that very seldom exists between believers, but it is what we long for and are made for. A normal group of people gathering can't experience the depth of this experience; only followers of Christ can. The Greek word *homothumadon* is usually translated in the Bible as "in one accord." It is a compound word made out of two words: *Homo* means "same, homogeneous, containing the same consistency"; and *thymus* means "passion, fieriness, fire, heat, a boiling forth, or aglow." *Homothumadon* is passionate enthusiasm. When the word is used in the different Bible texts, the presence of the Lord is there with all the believers who are one in spirit, one in heart with a unanimous passionate enthusiasm for the Lord and his direction. This is the oneness that Jesus prayed for in John 17.

In this situation in Acts, there is a oneness—the people were in one accord and had a fiery passion for what God was doing within them. They prayed passionately in one accord. We see this *homothumadon* in Acts 2:46: "they continued daily with one accord in the temple" (KJV). When the new believers gathered together hearing the disciples teaching, fellowshipping, praying, and breaking bread together, they were in one accord in their passion for Jesus, and wonderful things happened. The Spirit of God was burning inside them, so together they expressed their passionate heart and actions to God and one another.

When God shows up in a group of believers, it often becomes a safe place to be real and open with one another. We are all wired to want a safe place with Jesus, but we can also have it with one another. When God shows up with a strong teaching from the Word, or when there is very worshipful music, the people often want to turn their hearts and enthusiasm toward God in worship and toward each other in caring. When I teach from the Bible and God then uses it to impact people, they want to stay around afterward to visit and share. This is *homothumadon* in action. There is a sense of wonder and worship when believers connect around Jesus.

When individuals join a group of fellow believers who understand that they have been set free from sin and death by being "in Jesus," born of the Spirit and now in union with God their Father, oneness can happen. What was broken between God and man has been restored by the redemptive work of Jesus. The result of this union is lives changing from the inside out: there is a hunger to know Jesus and to continue in that relationship with him. Then there is the realization that if I am a son of God and in his family of God, these friends around me are now my brothers and sisters in Christ. There is Spirit oneness and a family oneness. "There is one body and one Spirit, just as you were called to one hope when you were called; one Lord, one faith, one baptism; one God and Father of all, who is over all and through all and in all." (Ephesians 4:4-6)

This fits. There is joy and peace and a sense that I was made for this. There can be for you, too. The awareness of others becomes spontaneous so that we refresh one another as we hang out. I have observed at the weekly men's fellowship and Bible study where I teach that when I really lift up Jesus and the men are moved toward him, afterward they want to hang around and fellowship with each other. Why? Through this oneness with God and by hearing truth, the men's knowledge of him increases, producing a deeper sense of knowing God that naturally expresses itself in oneness to fellow believers. It doesn't always work out that well, though: some weeks, the men walk out afterward without stopping to talk with one another, as if they hadn't been fed (spiritually). What was lost for us with what happened to Adam and Eve gets restored with this dynamic fellowship with God and fellow believers. On those occasions, it feels like the right time for a party. Let's celebrate with passion and in one accord, or *homothumadon*.

The fellowship in Acts 2:42-47 with one another was expressed with some powerful oneness words and phrases such as "all together," "everything in common," "met together," and "broke bread in homes." Eating a meal with someone can be one of the most personal and life-engaging experiences possible; to do it in your own home or sanctuary adds a new dimension. What a wonderful time to get rid of all agendas and have the physical needs met with food and drink as well as the relational need that God made us with—all coming together to connect with real life, including both the pains and the joys. There is trust, openness, where the atmosphere is right to connect. Then add the presence of Jesus. Perfect!

There is a reason Jesus has believers continuing to take the Lord's Supper together. Not only do we remember what Jesus did for us and preach the gospel to ourselves again, we also are engaging and being reminded of what God did for us and what we have as those who are in relationship with God. It is his Kingdom coming on earth, just as it is and will be in heaven. There is a synergy of fellowship around the Father-Son-Holy Spirit and those who are one with the Godhead, believers in Jesus.

This idea of *homothumadon* is a movement of enthusiasm for Jesus, and for Kingdom things, as well as for fellow believers. The translation of Acts 1:14 as "one accord" or in Acts 2:42 doesn't do justice to the word. *In "one accord"* could mean just being in agreement on where to eat dinner or in taking a ride together. There is far more passion and fire and enthusiasm for the Lord and his presence and direction that is expressed. Look at Acts 4:24: "And when they heard that, they lifted up their *voice to God with one accord* (emphasis mine) and said, 'Lord, thou *art* God, which hast made heaven, and earth, and the sea.'" The believers had seen the truth and reality of what Jesus had done and who he was; so they spontaneously joined together to share the truth. They understood from the disciples what Jesus was like and what he taught so that they could know, love, trust, obey, and praise him.

What did it mean to be in oneness with Jesus? They met in order to go deeper with Jesus and sharpen one another. Even later, Paul prayed for the believers in Romans 15:5-6, "May the God who gives endurance and encouragement give you the same attitude of mind toward each other that Christ Jesus had so that with one mind (*homothumadon*) and one voice you may glorify the God and Father of our Lord Jesus Christ." This is what was happening when believers gathered together. It is what God has for us as well. This is the oneness that Jesus prayed for in John 17. Let's get on it.

Before we leave Acts 2:42-47, let's look at the overflowing of this presence of God among the believers. They had everything in common: They met together in the temple courts, broke bread together in their homes, praised God together, and enjoyed favor of all the people. In a sense, they were having a party. I remember Tony Campolo, a professor of sociology, pastor, and public speaker, speaking on the subject of "The Kingdom of God is a Party." At parties we leave behind our worries, work, and obligations in order to celebrate. There is freedom to unwind, to laugh, and even to dance. I believe there was so much joy and fellowship in the Acts church that it truly was a party. Guess what? God added to their number daily of those being saved. The friends around these new believers wanted in on what they saw. Who wouldn't want to be part of that kind of fellowship and fun? The oneness between the Father-Son-Holy Spirit with believers was there, and the horizontal oneness between the believers was present.

I have experienced this with men many times in a Christian Leadership Concepts (CLC) group. We made a commitment to meet weekly for two years to study God's Word. We fellowshipped together with lots of fun and with laughter, while also being stretched and challenged with life issues and relationships among ourselves. There is something really special when a group of followers of Jesus is passionately pursuing him for the long haul. There is an eagerness to really know him and walk with him, as well as the desire to truly be in fellowship with each other. Prayers flow, people are cared for, spiritual growth takes place, and the Kingdom comes. There is an eagerness to pass this on to a hungry world.

While writing this book, I experienced something interesting. I was also reading a book for pleasure that I had picked up on display at the library, entitled *God's Double Agent* by Bob Fu. This Chinese man grew up in poverty but was smart enough to go to college. While there he visited Tiananmen Square to protest the Chinese government and its plans for the future, only to get singled out by the authorities and harassed. Through the persecution he became a follower of Jesus. I found his desire to know Jesus and to meet in a secret house church fascinating. When they met, there was so much enthusiasm and hunger for Jesus and strengthening from one to another that they realized they had to get together no matter the consequences. As a result, many came to the Lord. How awesome! It inspired me to yearn for that kind of fellowship. It sounded so much like what we looked at in Acts 2. It isn't complicated or exclusive, but dynamic; it is the reality God longs for us to experience.

Believers Experiencing Deep and Real Fellowship

"Behold how good and pleasant when brothers dwell together in unity." (Psalm 133) This is what fellowship is all about.

When this oneness is lived out among a body of believers, there is a "full measure of my joy within them." (John 17:13) Real fellowship is when this full joy is experienced. It is similar to the joy Jesus mentioned in John 15:11 and 16:24. There is joy by abiding in Jesus, the Vine that is deeper than happiness. It is from the Holy Spirit as a fruit but in some ways it is more. Joy is life and aliveness. All else is a pale substitute, and this aliveness only comes from being in Jesus. Joy is there when believers in one accord are in prayer, singing, serving one another, discovering truth together, or being reconciled to one another. God's Kingdom has come on earth, and all that are present and in oneness with Jesus and one another sense it.

Unfortunately, churches today don't look much like what I just described. Showing up at church once a week, looking at the back of someone's head, listening to a sermon, singing a few songs without thinking about the words, praying by just bowing one's head, and then telling the preacher "Good job," on the way out isn't very impactful or meaningful. We yearn for real relationships with God and each other, and most churches just aren't geared to do that.

We are designed as humans to interact on a deep level, encompassing the spiritual dimension and the relational dimension, which only followers of Jesus can have. Experiencing this closeness is indescribable and life changing. But it's not all roses, either. When fallen believers get together, we often fall off the wagon in many ways. That is part of it—loving one another enough to help a fallen brother or sister get back on the wagon. It is learning to deal with one another's differences in personality because of a family commitment that stands through thick and thin. Guess who is right in the middle, providing the power to deal with issues and the love and the unity? Jesus. He is the connector with the family oneness.

I would like to think that believers experience this oneness all the time. In a sense, they do, but it sometimes comes with issues and clashes. Actually, this conflict can help lead to greater oneness as followers of Jesus work through issues and challenge one another to excellences and oneness.

It is amazing how real life happens when six to fifteen people consistently get together over an extended period of a year or two. Many earth-shaking life issues happen in the form of money concerns, things at work, children or marriage situations, health changes, etc. Many groups have prayer requests on upcoming or current health issues. Sadly, people often play it safe, staying protective and shallow and boring and unreal. They miss out on an opportunity to go deeper by standing with one another and be real friends.

Let me challenge you not to settle for weak fellowship in your circles or in your church. Be a trailblazer and take this message forward. The best way to do this is for you to be a pacesetter by sharing your heart with the group concerning some personal issues. Also study Scripture or the lesson for the day beforehand and be prepared to take the group to a deeper level in knowing Jesus. In Appendix I, I will talk about setting up a group that will be effective in experiencing the things we talked about in this chapter.

Remember, as the facilitator, or leader, experiences a deep relationship with God, that experience will be seen and perceived by those in the group. They will see the passion for God and hear real-life encounters. They will long for that personal touch with God they see in the facilitator, and it will overflow to the group. Likewise when the group is connected on a deeper level, the relationship with Jesus will be influenced positively. Groups with a balance of fun, laughter, openness and digging deeply into the Bible and into God will experience the oneness Jesus prayed for in John 17.

⤝

Group Discussion Questions:

Hook: Could some of you tell about the best time of "church" or fellowship that you have ever experienced? Without being critical, share your desires and disappointments for fellowship.

1. Head. Summarize the truths around the prayer Jesus had about oneness for believers. How does that oneness relate to what he has with his Father and believers? What would that oneness look like in your church?

2. Head. Summarize the teaching of the Greek word *homothu-madon*. How and where have you, or have you not, experienced that kind of the presence of the Lord?

3. Heart. Without being critical, what has been your experience in small groups? How did these experiences help or hinder your relationship with Jesus?

4. Heart. Can anyone share an experience when you were in a group and the fellowship was so sweet and biblical that it helped you grasp the nature and relationship or oneness of God within the Father, Son, and Holy Spirit? How does the oneness-relationship that the Trinity experiences instruct believers' fellowship?

5. Heart. How do the five pillars of abiding seem to be applicable to what can take place in a fellowship as explained in the text?

6. Hand. As you compare and contrast 1 Thessalonians 1:2-3 with Revelation 2:3-4, what can you do to encourage the best of both churches in your group or this group?

7. Hand. How can your group be specific with the teaching from 1 Corinthians 12:12-26?

11

Sharing Life and Truth with New Friends

"We have left everything to follow you."
— Peter
MATTHEW 19:27
⁓

THIS BOOK IS ALL ABOUT RELATIONSHIPS. THE RELATIONSHIP WITH Jesus radically changes a person's life from one that was dull, meaningless, and crying out for direction and hope. Jesus is the life that brought light to men (John 1:4). This relationship is reality. The dullness of life and the enigmas of life begin to become clear in Jesus. When one is in that relationship with Jesus, life comes alive with vision and vitality, and produces life and joy. Jesus in someone's life begins to communicate what life is all about and what is worthwhile. How does someone transfer this wonderful life with Jesus to someone else? This transfer is about relationships and the truth. Very little happens outside relationships. We were made to be relational just like our Father and his Son were in relationship. He works through relationships and calls us to do the same.

Remember how God chose to communicate with mankind? It wasn't with a fly-over plane like you see on the beach advertising the big event of the week. His plan was to come live among us. God with us—the incarnation. "The Word became flesh." (John 1:14) Jesus lived that game plan out with his disciples. As you remember, when religious authorities asked the disciples, who were unschooled and ordinary men, about Jesus, they basically responded that they

135

had been "with Jesus" and that is who and what they saw in their lives. Likewise, we are living out our relationship with Jesus now.

"In the past God spoke to our forefathers through the prophets and various other ways, but in the last days he has spoken to us by his Son . . ." (Hebrews 1:1-2). Jesus, the Word of Life, was right in the disciples' presence so they could see him, touch him, and walk and talk with him (1 John 1:1-4). We get to have fellowship with Jesus, too, meaning we all have things in common: life, heritage, intimacy with the Father, and complete joy. It is all relational.

Out of this deep, personal relationship with Jesus, we join in fellowship with other believers in Jesus to enjoy him and encourage one another in our walk with him. Thankfully, God has appointed us to take the relationship we have with him and other believers to those who are outside that fellowship. It's exciting to include them, to get to be a part of the relational transfer. It is also very scary; boldness is required, and the possibility of rejection is always the next conversation away. It is good to know that God has the very way you and I entered into a relationship with God.

Paul captures the process in one short verse: "The things you have heard me say in the presence of many witnesses, entrust to reliable men who will also be qualified to teach others." (2 Timothy 2:2) You will notice that there are four parties there: Paul, the writer; Timothy, the recipient; reliable people; and others to be taught. I picture the Olympics where the 4 x 100 relay is run, and the baton is passed from one sprinter to the next while running full speed. The training and timing are essential, as they all have to work together. It is a process that is dynamic and fluid. In many ways, that is a picture of how Paul transferred this life with Jesus to Timothy by telling him the truth. This baton was passed down for about two thousand years so that eventually it got to me. You were involved in a similar process of seeing Jesus and believing in him. Hopefully I am passing you part of the truth-baton in this book. As believers, we have the baton passed to us.

The baton-passing experience started with Jesus and the disciples. Jesus came to earth, and he invited twelve men to join him. They, along with Barnabas, passed the gospel-baton to Paul. Paul passed it to Timothy and after hundreds of years, it eventually got to Jim Rayburn, who started Young Life in 1941. Someone in Knoxville then passed it on to Charlie Scott, who passed it on to me. Every one of us has a story of someone who passed us the baton. Now we get to relationally pass the gospel-baton.

What's neat about this is that this is not some program I'm trying to recruit you to. It is just about sharing life with a friend. It is an "as you go" relational building experience. Think about where you spend about 99 percent of your awake time: work, home, and play. You know friends in all those places and have a great opportunity to pass the baton . . . naturally, with nothing forced, no salesmanship needed. The essence of what I am talking about is both biblical and fun. Remember, it is an "as you go" relational experience.

Paul wrote a letter to the Thessalonians, chapter 1:5, recapturing what they had experienced in the past through his relationship with them. There are two main points to focus on. Paul wrote (emphasis mine), ". . . .our *gospel* came to you. . . . you know how *we lived among you* . . . " There are two essential components in passing the baton to your friend so that he or she can experience this personal, intimate relationship with Jesus. Remember, Paul got it from the disciples and Barnabas, and they got it from Jesus. If it was God's plan for Jesus and Paul's plan, maybe we should make it our plan, too.

An "As You Go" Experience with an Olympic Athlete from a Foreign Country

This is an unlikely friendship with a man I met while on the staff of Young Life on the island of Bermuda. (Somebody had to "suffer" for the Lord there!) While playing basketball at a local high school, the coach said I needed to meet a particular person because he said we had a lot in common.

I introduced myself to this man and set up an appointment, wondering what we had in common other than basketball. It was soon apparent that we really had nothing in common except our concern for teenagers. He was black, I was white. He was an agnostic,

I was a Christian. He was a former two-time Olympic decathlon competitor and European decathlon champion at one point. My "athletic strength" was watching a lot of football on TV. I was born in the US, and he was from another country. I knew he wouldn't be ready to help with Young Life at this point, so I decided to just be a friend and hopefully find a similar interest or common ground. We had an awesome conversation that laid the ground work for friendship. I prayed that would soon happen.

Out of our developing friendship, he revealed that he was a squash player and invited me to a game. He didn't tell me that he was the No. 4-ranked squash player in Bermuda. I asked if he would teach me, and as you can imagine, it was no contest. However, squash is played on a court similar to handball. Interestingly, I had brought two pairs of handball gloves with me when I moved from the States. Wisely, I offered to teach him a sport I could play—handball. With my "know-how" and his athletic ability, we had some great games. That fun common-ground activity opened the door to talk and share life together afterward.

One evening he invited me over to eat some of his famous cooked liver and onions (when I was growing up, liver was my least-favorite dish). This gave us more time to talk and find out what the other believed. Over the months, a great friendship developed, and God opened the door for me to talk to him about the Truth, Jesus, and life. He had some hard questions and disagreed with many of my views. Fortunately, we both accepted each other, right where we were. We just enjoyed being together to laugh and discuss life issues. It helped that both of us cared about teenagers. Eventually, the gospel began to make sense to him, and he put his trust in Jesus. Later we teamed up to start a coffeehouse for teens, which we called Psychedelic Fish. (I'll leave that story for another time.)

My experience with my newfound friend showed me that through the work of the Holy Spirit, prayer, time, love, common-ground activities, and discussion, God could use me with anyone. Sadly, my friend would die at just forty-six years of age, about fifteen years after he began his relationship with Jesus, leaving behind two daughters. Recently, out of my love for him and our friendship, I tried to track down his girls, whom I hadn't seen since they were about two to four years old. I found them in Sweden about three years ago, and we have corresponded and sent Christmas cards and gifts to each other. I have had the opportunity to tell them about their dad and our friendship, as well as how he began a relationship with Jesus.

Two Key Principles for Helping Our Friends Join Our Fellowship

1. Living Among

The thought of establishing a friendship with someone who is very different from you and is an unbeliever in Jesus is both exciting and frightening. My goal for you is for that experience to be fun, natural, and energizing. Unfortunately, from my experience, when there is talk of doing evangelism, most people I know break out in a cold sweat and the walls of resistance go up. Evangelism is a door-closer for many. At the same time, I think most believers would love to see their friends and family have a personal relationship with God, and you can be instrumental in that process. Some of the most excited I have seen people get is when someone close to them enters into a relationship with Jesus. Let's approach this passing of the baton with a positive attitude and an expectation of seeing our friends embrace a God relationship, as in the process we learn to trust God more.

Our desire in reaching out to people whom we either meet along the way (as-you-go relationships) or whom we already have in our circle of influence is to become friends with them by sharing life together, such that they can sense we truly value them and want to be with them. Another desire is to share the gospel when God opens the door and the circumstance is appropriate. In order to do this, there must be ways to connect as one gets to know the other in a natural and spontaneous friendship. It is an experience where we establish common interest or common ground. It is not any different from any good friendship. In order to be friends, you have to spend time together, and in order to do that, there need to be activities you can do together, both in good times and bad. These activities can range from uncomfortable interactions in the aftermath of a tragedy to fun events that are energizing and purposeful. Either way, life is shared, and friendships are developed.

Again, our models are Jesus and Paul. Recall some of the experiences Jesus had with his disciples. He hung out on Lake Galilee, fished with them, ate with them, and even calmed the storm while they watched. He got into their world as they walked through life together for three and a half years. They saw one other as friends. Along the way, the disciples saw people healed, and together with Jesus they also walked through grain fields, made bathroom pit stops, hiked hills and mountains, and prayed together—just everyday kinds of stuff. No doubt they laughed together, cried together, rejoiced together, and shared amazement at what God did in their midst through Jesus. The key is that they were together.

Paul did exactly the same thing in his life-sharing means of operating. Take note of his writing in 1 Corinthians 9:19, "Though I am free and belong to no man, I make myself a slave to everyone, to win as many as possible." He went on to say, "To the Jews I became like a Jew, and to the Gentile, I became like a Gentile." He became "like" these other people in order to share life with them and break down barriers.

There are barriers to relationships that we all must live out. Think of the people you naturally shy away from for various reasons—different socio-economics, racial differences, age gaps. There seems to be a big chasm between us and them, making it very tough to build a natural friendship. Regardless, it is our responsibility, like it was for Paul, to build a bridge of friendship to them. We can't expect them to come to our strange world; we must find out what they are interested in and join them.

Close your eyes and try to see the word picture of "building a bridge of friendship" to others unlike you. Bridge building takes time and work in order for you to get to the point where you can walk across it naturally. Paul and Jesus were masterful at practicing that principle. Generally speaking, without bridge building we don't have much of a chance to do or say anything to those on the other side. As best you can, be like Paul and become "slave" to your friends by becoming "like" them, truly identifying with them. That is what I experienced when my Young Life leader, Charlie Scott, came to my school, hung out with me at the smoking pit, learned my name, and sought to do fun things with me. It got my attention.

Young Life founder Jim Rayburn called this approach "winning the right to be heard." Notice the three key components of that phrase:

Winning: We have to work at it with prayers and strategy and time spent with them.

The right: We can't just charge into their lives and dump our good news on them. None of us likes a pushy salesperson or an uninvited person in our home.

Heard: We have good news to share and we need and want receptive ears. This is establishing common ground, or bridge building, or becoming a slave, what Jesus did by incarnational living—coming in the flesh to live among us.

There is a natural relationship-building process. Establishing common ground or interest can help you be proactive with your friends. As you share life together, get to know them, care about them, build trust, and maybe present truth to them as God's leads.

- Share your life with them. Hang out with them and accept them right where they are. Friends do that. Get to know them. This is as basic as knowing their name, interest, history, dreams, family, career, and what and where they like to eat. Eating a meal together at a restaurant or in your home is one of the greatest ways to hang out, relax, and enjoy one another's company. In that time you will discover what they believe politically, socially, and spiritually. They could have strong objections to Christianity and religion in general, or could have some interest. You will not know without spending time and asking questions, but don't ask too many and definitely not rapid-fire. Some will have objections to Christianity, like "Why would God allow bad things to happen to good people?" or, "Religion is for weak people." Picture these skeptical friends running the 110-meter hurdles, with each hurdle a barrier to their coming face-to-face with Jesus. In a natural and clear way, address their questions and issues in open discussion. Ask them what they mean by certain comments but definitely don't let it get to a debate or argument. Accommodate their questions, and don't get defensive. While you are getting to know them, and they you, try to discern their needs that God could address. Presenting the Truth at their point of need is essential and more effective than a blanket presentation; needs lay the groundwork needed in order to present a solution, the Truth, i.e. the Gospel.

- When we really do want to know them and let them know us, it communicates loud and clear that they are valuable—that they are worth getting to know and to become friends with. It is a time to let them know you as well, allowing the relationship to be a two-way street. Your being vulnerable helps them to be open. Don't appear to have it all together; guess what? None of us do. Care for them and seek to really love them. No one is lining up to be judged, but they are lining up to be cared for. Spending time with them and sincerely trying to get to know them sends the message that you care for them. They are important. To care and love when they are different from you in lifestyle, beliefs, and any other difference singles you out from most of the people they are around. When you care, they will begin to share more and reveal their life and needs with you. That opens the door to pray and maybe share the truth. Trust them and they will trust you. Basically, you are communicating with them that you are trustworthy. Showing trustworthiness can start by showing that you are trusting them, perhaps letting them pick up your mail for you if you're going to be away for a while or confiding in them some of your own life issues and even letting *them* minister to or mentor *you* in some fashion. Again, there's that two-way street. If they offer to cut your grass while you are on vacation, go for it. You don't always have to be the caregiver. Now that you have been involved in some ongoing basics with your friend, you will likely start seeing opportunities to share the gospel. I call it "appropriate sharing." A few begin a relationship with Jesus through confrontation or a direct approach, but most begin that relationship after building a bridge of friendship. Before we go there, let me tell you about another of my "as you go" encounters.

An "As You Go" Experience with an Inner-City Family

One day there was a knock at the door of my office. We kept the door locked because we were in a risky area near downtown Nashville. Waiting at the door was a man who appeared to be about thirty years old with his arm in a sling. He told me that he was disabled and needed food for his family. Being the suspicious type, a little street-wise, and assuming he planned on buying liquor, I told him no. He pulled out a medical form that said he was truly disabled. I wasn't convinced and asked if I could call the doctor who signed the form. He agreed. Interestingly, I talked directly to the doctor who said this man had cut an artery, veins, and nerves in an accident. I felt pretty bad about doubting him.

At that point, I began looking for an agency that helps people who are like him in need, to provide him with food. I didn't realize I needed a PhD in government systems to get help—talk about phone tag and a game of runaround! Finally, I made a helpful connection, and I took him to his apartment. Entering the living room, I saw a two-seater couch and an old TV sitting on an old plastic milk basket. That was it! No lights, nothing! We passed through the bedroom where two single mattresses rested on the floor. That was it! Then on to the kitchen where there was a stove and refrigerator, but no table or chairs.

I didn't make it to the back bedroom. I was blown away. This family was in great need! He was out of work, disabled, and as I later learned, he had little education. His wife worked in house-keeping at a local motel. They had three children and had been married for twelve years.

I remembered about six months earlier when I was walking from the tire store back to my office, seeing many men from the Union Rescue Mission lying down or standing on the street. I prayed, "Lord, I hurt for these men, but I don't know what to do. I wish there was a family I could get involved with and have a longer and bigger impact." It appeared this family was an answer to that prayer. In ways that I couldn't have imagined before meeting this man, I have helped them with jobs, cars, food, clothes, and getting them to church. The toughest part was seeing their sixteen-year-old daughter die after childbirth in a major hospital and then speaking at her funeral.

After being involved with this family for several years, I finally had a chance to lay out the gospel and see the husband commit his life to Christ. That family is now actively involved in a church. Twenty years later, I am still standing with one daughter with her two kids. As for the son who was born as his mother died in childbirth, I had the privilege of watching him graduate from high school and commit his life to Jesus. As I write this, I am now trying to help get him into college.

One day while visiting someone at the hospital, I ran into the wife (I had helped her get a housekeeping job there). While we were visiting, her supervisor came up to us, and she introduced me by saying, "This is my friend." That was one of the highest compliments I have ever received. To be called a friend is about as good as it gets. This was a friendship on a two-way street. Awesome!

Now back to the main points that Jesus and Paul used.

2. Sharing the Gospel

"Our gospel came to you not simply with words, but also with power, with the Holy Spirit and with deep conviction. You know how we lived among you for your sake" (1 Thessalonians 1:5). Here is a good picture of what happens: the gospel needs to be shared with words, not just living a good life. Sharing the gospel also needs to be accompanied by God's power because we can never make a conversion happen in someone's life on our own. That is God's job. And note the importance of living among our friends because we care. It is a life impacting a life.

Once you have developed a good solid friendship with your unbelieving friends, it is time to begin to think about this question: How do I cross that bridge of friendship and share the gospel? Remember, the Father must draw them to Jesus (John 6:46), but you and I have a part—sharing the gospel. We never want to be content just hanging out and being friendly, even though that may be all God would have us do in a particular instance. When we really love and care for someone, we can't rest until we have made an effort to present the gospel to them. Paul sums this point up on when he says, "We loved you so much we are willing to share not only the gospel but our lives as well because you had become so dear to us." (I Thessalonians 2:8) Isn't that awesome? Those are the exact actions we need to be taking—loving them and presenting the gospel.

A metaphor that helps me with this tandem process is dancing with a partner. It takes two to tango. You knew that, right? Someone initiates the dance when the music comes on; then you get on the dance floor, where you hold hands as the feet start moving. Around the dance floor you go, making adjustments to the other dancer and the music. One leads and the other follows. There is give and take as well as conversation as you go. It is fun, relaxed, and intentional. It also is very relational. There is a balance between talking about convictions and showing compassion, or a balance between grace and truth. When we get too rigid or mechanical in dancing, it just doesn't flow and isn't much fun. When we step on our partner's shoes, it breaks the rhythm, just like when we come on too strong or are unequipped. There is awkwardness in dancing just like there is in sharing the gospel. Don't worry; that's part of it.

An "As You Go" Experience
with an Influential Businessman

One night I was with about ten couples together in a friend's home, where we were having a discussion on life and God. Half the couples were followers of Jesus. In that hour we discussed a number of topics. It wasn't Q&A time but just an open forum that I was facilitating. It was full of energy and emotions but no anger or argumentative spirits. We were all seeking truth.

As we ended, an influential businessman who had been quite engaged rushed up to talk with me one on one. He wanted some answers, not just opinions. I had my Bible but choose not to use it because I wanted to keep the discussion going. I suggested to this man that we have lunch together sometime. We set an appointment to meet, and at that lunch we had a great discussion relevant to where he was coming from theologically and practically. That lunch was followed by about four or five more get-togethers. I wasn't in any hurry to try to present the gospel because we were enjoying discussing many topics and two or three times he sought to get a handle on the truth. We developed a good friendship.

On the fifth meeting, he asked a deep and thought-provoking question: "What is it going to cost me if I commit my life to Jesus?" Being a successful businessman, he was thinking bottom line. At that moment I felt God give me an answer, but I was sweating bullets because I didn't want to come across as too pushy or to hold back out of fear. Still, I told him, "It cost Jesus his life; it will cost you your life." I didn't soft coat things, believing he wanted an honest, real answer, not just a nice lukewarm response to smooth things over. He said he was ready to make that commitment. Today, he is walking with Jesus, involved in his church and community. God has burdened him with a ministry in our city to prisoners. My friend has been chairman of the board and a spokesman for the ministry, where others are joining him to make a significant impact.

I trust you see all the elements from finding common ground to caring, as well as the slow, natural process. With God being in charge, there is no reason to rush and try to make things happen. It is fun. By the way, I don't think I have the gift of evangelism. I just love to hang out with people, being their friend, and I do know the gospel and feel comfort presenting it in an attractive manner. God does the rest.

There are three important steps to take as you are in this fluid relationship with a friend whom you are in the process of leading to Christ:

- Pray the gospel. "Devote yourselves to prayer, being watchful and thankful. And pray for us, too, that God may open a door for our message, so that we may proclaim the mystery of Christ, for which I am in chains. Pray that I may proclaim it clearly, as I should" (Colossians 4:2-4). This calls on God to prepare the path, prepare this person's heart, and prepare us to present. It is a God thing. This isn't necessarily a quick prayer, but let it be specific and intentional; it can be as long as it takes to do what God is calling you to do in this "dance." Always be watchful for God opening a door for you to take the next step, and be thankful when you see movement. It is a picture of all three of us being engaged in this dance process: our friend, us, and God. He is leading the dance and playing the music. The Spirit of God is at work convicting us of sin, righteousness, and judgment. Without him moving, our labor is in vain.

- Know the gospel. You can pretty well count on it that your friends don't know the gospel. We assume they do, but I have found that few people know the gospel. They may know a bit about church and Christian rules and how they have been treated by Christians, but that is typically about all. Oh, they might have a media-sourced opinion of what being a Christian is, but mainly that is incorrect. Maybe they know he performed miracles and was a teacher, but usually not much else.

I believe many unbelievers have rejected the wrong Jesus. I want them to truly know the facts about the real Jesus; our responsibility is to communicate that to them. Unfortunately, many, if not most, believers don't know the real Jesus or the gospel. Yes, you heard me right. Can you lay out the gospel in a clear manner so that your friend can understand it? If the gospel is fuzzy to you, think about what it is to your friend. Paul said he was not ashamed of the gospel (Roman 1:16). But how often are we ashamed of it? The main reason is that we don't know the gospel or how to present it.

Every follower of Jesus should not only know the gospel but be able to communicate it by using your own personal experience of receiving Jesus to explain it. For example, in about five minutes or less, I can relate how I heard in great detail that God loved me, and just how much that meant to me even though I was a sinner separated from him. My sin cut me off from God and I needed a Savior. Jesus came to live among us and to die for us to make the sacrifice required by God because our good works don't suffice. By faith, I trusted Jesus with my life by believing in him and receiving him, thus becoming one of his followers or sons.

- Use a tailor-made gospel. In this "dance" with our friends, we can tailor the truth we present to make it fit them. Let's go back to the Colossians passage (4:2-6) in which we are instructed to make the most of every opportunity and know how to "answer everyone." To me that means answering each one in a manner that would be spot-on with them—not a blanket answer but one that would communicate with them.

As we listen to them, they will express their needs, and that gives us the opportunity to speak to them about how Jesus meets those needs. For example, someone might tell you how he feels distant from God, so your gospel message can center on the personal nature of God and how he wants to draw close to us. Or someone might have fears about life or feeling unloved or directionless. Jesus addresses all of those, and you can emphasize Jesus's meeting our personal needs as he presented the truth and plan of salvation. Jesus had this with the blind man in John 9:1-7: he dealt with the physical need and later came back to meet his spiritual needs in verses 35-41. Jesus did a similar approach with the woman at the well, as well as with the one caught in adultery. It takes a combination of active listening, asking questions, and knowing the many ways Jesus meets everyone right where they are. It always amazes me how unique each person's encounter with Jesus is and what it was about Jesus that attracted them. In every case, Jesus met them right where they were with the truth.

There comes a point where you should ask them if they are ready to pray and commit their lives to Jesus. This, too, can be awkward. I am not convinced my way is the right way to do this, but I'm going to share my general approach anyway, because I do feel confident that God has used me in the following manner:

- I ask permission from them to lay out the way they can be in a personal relationship with Jesus.

- If they say yes, I like to draw out a picture on a napkin or a piece of paper with a visual map. It shows mankind on one side of a chasm, like the Royal Gorge in Canyon City, Colorado, and God on the other side. The chasm represents sin separating us from God. At the Royal Gorge, the example I use, it is a thousand feet across and a thousand feet down. I tell how we might try on our own to jump across that chasm, only to get about ten to twenty feet out from the edge, and then it's a thousand feet straight down. We can't make it on our own. I parallel this to our efforts of good works such as giving, serving, and going to church. I tell them crossing that chasm is a gift of grace from God. By the way, for all of these points I make, I have a scripture reference to support what I am presenting. One I sometimes use is Ephesians 2:8-10. "It is by grace you are saved, not by works." Then I show how Jesus's death is the bridge across the chasm, so I draw the cross touching each side.

- Finally, I ask if they would like to pray to receive Jesus. If so, I then quickly lay out the major points and tell them they can pray those, if that is their heart's desire. I tell them they can pray when we are in my car, or when they are driving back to work, or that night before they go to sleep. If they want to pray right away, I suggest that I pray a brief prayer followed by their prayer out loud. My thought is that verbalizing it helps the person to solidify the decision in front of the one pointing them to Jesus. It is not essential to start the relationship with Jesus.

• If they do pray and surrender their lives to Jesus, I talk about follow-up and what the next steps are for truly walking with and following Jesus. I am committed to seeing them become disciples and not just converts. There is no command in Scripture to make converts.

In summary, I regard this process as adding links in a chain. Picture a chain with fifty links; the first would be the initial thing God used to communicate the gospel with someone and each of the other links would be other encounters that God used. Link No. 50 would be when they prayed to commit their life to Jesus. Link No. 10 could be their grandmother praying for them specifically. No. 23 could be attending a Chris Tomlin concert; No. 37 could be a believer meeting some need; No. 41 could be a book they read, such as *Mere Christianity*; No. 42 could be reading from the Gideon Bible in their hotel room. There is no real pattern because God is orchestrating the process. He's using who he wants to use in the way he wants. Knowing he is in control sure relaxes me; I don't have to make anything happen with my friend, just be obedient to God's leading. It is truly exciting.

There is urgency, though. Jesus makes a statement that gets my attention. He gives the most famous verse from scripture (John 3:16), "For God so loved the world that he gave his only begotten Son that whoever believes in him shall not perish but have eternal life." Two verses later, in 18, he says, "Whoever does not believe is condemned *already* . . . " (emphasis mine). That means right now, not necessarily just at death. He goes further in verse 36: "But whoever rejects the Son will not see life, for God's wrath *remains* (emphasis mine) in him." If God is prompting you to share the gospel, don't wait!

An "As You Go" Experience with a Young Female Lawyer

One day while working out at the local YMCA, I had a casual conversation with a woman in her thirties who was working out as well, and we had some casual conversation. The next week I was at Starbucks and ran into her and her boyfriend. We all introduced ourselves and engaged in some small talk. In the conversation, it came out that we all had a few things in common: working out at the YMCA with workouts, coffee, and bicycling. Now we had three common ground areas to build on. Frankly I wasn't thinking of building on any of them. But we kept running into each other at Starbucks and catching up.

As the weather got nicer, we decided to bike together. This was enjoyable and we were beginning to get to know each other, becoming friends on a very basic level. I remember speaking at a business breakfast to which I invited them, and she came. Later I invited her boyfriend to be my guest at a Titans football game, to which he gladly came along. Later my wife and I invited the two of them for dinner. That was when we really began to get to know each other. They asked about my history and vice versa. It was a fun night, and we found more things that we had in common as we all shared more about our lives.

Then one morning when I ran into them again at Starbucks, I asked how it was going and she mentioned a tough situation at work. As her friend, I just listened. I made myself available if she wanted to talk more. She texted back that she would like to visit and came to my house the following Saturday morning, where my wife and I greeted her. After about an hour of hearing her situation, I started drawing on a piece of paper, explaining how she could have a personal relationship with God. Yes, I used the Royal Gorge example, sharing the main points of the gospel. I explained that God loved her and wanted to be involved in her life to bless, guide, forgive, and strengthen and other factors that applied to her life and what she had shared. Also, I told her about how sin does separate us from God, much like the chasm at the Royal Gorge. She had been in church but never seen the relationship as very personal. We talked about God's sacrifice for her with the death of Christ and how she could pray and trust her life to him. As you can imagine, she did pray and commit her life to Jesus, right there in my sunroom. We discipled her a bit and invited her to come to our church, where she now is growing and maturing rapidly in her relationship with Jesus. I think it is important to note that I have kept my wife involved at all levels. It is too easy to get off focus. This young woman now calls me her spiritual daddy. I am blessed to be that. By the way, she is sure faster than I am on the bike.

Group Discussion Questions:

Hook: Would a few of you tell about your joys and successes or your fears and failures in trying to share the gospel with someone?

1. Head. Would a few in the group connect the dots on the baton pass in your conversion experience? Be honest; can you truly tell how you begin a relationship with Christ and what the relationship is really like today?

2. Head. Discuss the meaning and process of "winning the right to be heard" with a friend. Talk about how it works, why it is appropriate, and why it can be awkward. How and why is the approach so countercultural to what we have been taught?

3. Heart. Why is the "in your face" approach so ineffective and so uncomfortable?

4. Heart. In Matthew 28:19, Jesus says to go make disciples. The "go" really means "as you go" in life, share life with friends or contacts, seeking to win the right to be heard. How might this feel more natural and motivating to you? How is this connected to the "dance" of relational building and sharing the gospel?

5. Hand. Would you explain the plan of salvation in a clear, brief manner?

6. Hand. Can you share where you are in putting a gospel-link in the life of someone you are in contact with, or someone you would like to begin the process with?

Appendix A

Establishing a Oneness Group with Friends

"If I just touch his clothes, I will be healed."
— The woman with a blood issue
JOHN 9:25

~~~

AS I HAVE SHARED, SOMETHING POWERFUL AND SPECIAL HAPPENS when a small group of ten to twelve believers (or even smaller) commits to being together for a long period of time to dig into the Word of God and share life together. It is a picture of what Jesus did with the twelve disciples over three and a half years. Life issues pushed them to God and toward each other. They learned to experience God and to practice oneness in diversity. It is a hands-on, experiential dynamic that results in transformation for individuals and bonding among the group members. It is all about relationships with God and one another, and the ultimate purpose of the group.

The relationship with God isn't just about me and him, simply us hanging out together. The greatest commandment and the summary of the entire Bible is to love the Lord with all your heart, mind, and soul, and to love your neighbor as yourself. It is truly all about relationships. It is what Jesus prayed for in John, chapters 14-17. These experiences of bringing believers together don't just happen by assigning a certain number to a group, or picking a topic and then asking people to sign up. This seems to be the tendency in many churches or fellowship groups, the old-fashioned way. All that does is produce groups that are miserable to be a part of. This clearly hinders the fellowship with one another and doesn't enhance the relationship with God.

In this appendix, I will share with you what I learned from Jesus and his twelve disciples and what I have been doing with men and women for decades. I am a "groupie" who sees the true value of experiencing life together with Jesus as the center.

In Acts 2:42-46, we see the new believers of Jesus right after his resurrection and how they incorporated this discipleship process. Here the church sought to become disciples of Jesus by sharing life together and discovering the truth of Jesus together. They did this by praying together, eating, sharing adventures, learning from the twelve disciples of Jesus, looking into the Scriptures, meeting each other's needs, affirming, exercising accountability, following leadership, and calling forth one another's gifts. They pointed one another to the Truth, Jesus.

In starting a discipleship group, your prime emphasis should be on growing closer to, and deeper in your relationship with Jesus and instilling that same desire into your group's participants. Paul described it well in Philippians 3:10: "I want to know Christ and the power of his resurrection . . ." This is the motivation, the only real reason to get in a group. Other motivations, such as wanting a group of friends to hang out with, or to develop self-discipline, or to start a men's group, a women's group, or a multiracial group are noble causes, but they aren't the highest purpose. It's easy to do groups but still miss out on Jesus.

It Is All about Relationships

It is easy to talk about relationships with God and others and even read about them in the Bible, but they are meant to be lived out in your "as you go" life. Don't pass over this "as you go" idea. This is relational in the sense that people are Spirit-led; it isn't by formula. There is a spontaneous, Spirit-led planned informality. When God came up with his strategy to take fallen man to a saving relationship with Jesus, he knew it was a lifestyle to be lived out, and it needed to be centered on his Son and his disciples.

156

God could have chosen a number of ways to accomplish his goals. One could have been to train people in an academic setting or even by doing it online, if available, or just by self-discovery or via a do-it-yourself approach. (My older brother is a dentist. Once I had an appointment with him, and he told me I needed a crown. I asked how much would it cost, and he said $895. I went ballistic! He excused himself and came back with a small kit saying it was a "do-it-yourself-kit" and it was only $29.95.) Today's method seems to be the do-it-yourself approach in which someone comes to Jesus at an event and is left to disciple himself by sitting in the pew or winging it on his own. That usually doesn't work.

As we know, Jesus came to live among mankind. He invited twelve men to be his disciples in whom he would invest his life for a little more than three years. Sure, there were times he spoke to large crowds and even conducted one-on-one teaching in much the same way he did with the rich young ruler and the man born blind. However, his preferred strategy in making an impact while on earth—and even thousands of years later—was to invest in a few good men and women. At first glance, it looks almost ineffective, extremely slow, and very limited in impact. In the long run, though, it was his only strategy.

Unfortunately, the church has tried to shortcut the plan and focus on church activity, evolving into an organization that is more like a social club instead of something that fulfills Jesus's purpose. There is value to corporate worship, preaching and teaching, family programs, buildings, and singing, but are these alone effective? What do you think? If cars come off the assembly line and don't work, people stop buying them, and the maker tries to solve the problem. Why doesn't the church wake up and do the same?

Let me focus on making disciples in a small group setting and discussing how Jesus did it. Disciple-making is about relationships. First, the group and each individual seek to grow in their relationship with Jesus and become like him. This is all covered earlier here. It is not about religious activity, doing things to impress others, or striving toward a standard to produce pride, failure, or guilt-induced living in the followers. It's all about how we are going deeper with

Jesus, a personal relationship incorporating the Father-son, Friend-friend, and Bridegroom-bride aspects.

The five pillars of relationship are essential. A disciple seeks to know Jesus or God. What are the facts that need to be grasped, and how can one really have a personal, ongoing encounter with Jesus? This is where the group always comes back to the Bible, the revealed Word of God, to get direction. Once the members better understand more and more truths from the Bible, they will not only know Jesus on a deeper level, but will want to pursue him in a passionate way. The group is meant to be the catalyst in nudging individuals and the group toward Jesus. This relationship goes further in learning to trust, obey, and praise Jesus, because it is all really about Jesus.

Second, the relationship among the members is essential to the health of the group because the members are the source for learning about Jesus. The relationship among group members is not the top priority, but just as God values relationship, he wants us to be vibrantly connected to one another. Very little transformation takes place outside a group. There is tremendous value in meeting with God alone, say, if you are on a hike, reading in his Word in privacy, or fasting. In fact those one-on-ones are essential for growth. From my experience, though, there is a reason Jesus came here with the intent of bringing together a group, and to encourage and challenge us in our walk with him; it's what the proverb refers to as "iron sharpening iron."

A lone antelope is the one picked off by the lion. God's design is for us is not to be in isolation, but to be in fellowship with one another, spurring on one another to love and do good deeds (Hebrews 10:24-25). Ecclesiastes 4:8-12 reveals that two are better than one, and two can defend themselves, and a cord of three strands is not quickly broken. Not only does a group help one another grow and survive, but they also push each other to Jesus. Where two or more are gathered in Jesus's name, he shows up in a big way (Matthew 18:20).

Third, the group needs to have the Bible as its foundation for study and discussion, as it is the revealed Word of God. The Bible is the authority. One can't stay on track in pursuing Jesus without the Bible, because it preserves what he spoke to men and women in those times that he revealed his heart, his mind, and his ways. To think that the Bible had more than forty authors from many walks of life—from fishermen to kings—and was written mainly in two languages over a period of fifteen hundred years across two continents, with *one* central theme is evidence that God orchestrated its writing and protected the reliability and authenticity of the content. While Adam and Eve disobeyed God in Genesis 3, resulting in separation from God, the sixty-six books of the Old and New Testament have the message of being in a right relationship with God.

A healthy, impactful group has two main components: the relationships of the members and the content that is discussed and applied. Therefore, the content can vary from group to group. It can be pure Bible study looking at a particular book, or a topical study from Scripture, or a systematic theological study of a contemporary Christian book. When using a particular book for study, though, often I see groups evaluating the author more than focusing on what the author says about truth and walking with Jesus. This is a smoke screen to avoid going deeper and drawing near Jesus. These books chosen for group study must be biblically based and then read with constructive criticism, not just in a manner of evaluating the author's style or language. All studies should follow the Bereans' example, in that they received Paul's message with great eagerness, and they examined the Scriptures every day to see if what Paul said was true (Acts 17:11).

In mentoring Timothy, Paul challenges him to be a workman who correctly handles the Word of truth. This should involve studying, listening, memorizing, reading, and, at the right time, teaching the Word. When life issues affecting group members arise, the group as a whole, along with the leader, has a responsibility to push toward the final authority and discern what the Bible says. This takes genuine commitment. Many groups don't come to the meeting prepared; they end up only sharing from their past experience, which might be stale or unbiblical. Outside preparation is essential so that each individual can encounter Jesus before coming to the meeting.

Our culture is not only moving away from a solid biblical base of knowledge and understanding; it is outright rejecting absolutes and becoming more relative, compromising biblical truths in the process. Our culture is becoming more and more secular, making man, not God, the final answer. This postmodern culture needs the Truth from God's Word. To follow Jesus, a disciple must know him and love him, and only by obeying Jesus can a disciple then truly trust him. Without the Scriptures, one person's ideas are just as good as another's, and chaos will follow as each one does what is right in their own eyes (Judges 21:25).

The fourth key component of a group is to deal with life issues. The members must be real and vulnerable. The facilitator should keep the discussion relevant to what participants are presently experiencing. The truth of the Bible addresses all issues that we face in this life. The facilitator's role is to provide a safe place where all can express their thoughts and feelings about their lives and about the Bible or the topic being looked at. The facilitator comes to the group with a game plan and is led and empowered by the Spirit, and also seeks to be sensitive to the participants' concerns and issues. If not, the group time will be a compartmentalized experience where most theorize on the Bible, but don't apply it to their lives. In fact current issues many times become the main focus and, therefore, an opportunity to allow the Bible to speak to us on real-life issues. If the facilitator is prepared for the meeting and aware of what is happening with the participants, he/she can be flexible and led by the Spirit so that truth and life collide. Getting the right answer or covering the content that the leader has planned isn't the goal. The goal is engaging the group with the truth in the Bible and the truth or reality of life.

Some of these life issues are pretty routine. The question is, are we as leaders going to be real and vulnerable? Are we ready to reveal our own feelings and thinking that cause us to turn to God? So many groups operate on the surface level, staying within one's comfort zone. That offers little growth among group members.

As a facilitator of many groups, I don't always ask the right questions to get people to open up. I can have an atmosphere in which the participants trust one another enough to open up, but there's no guarantee that will happen on any given day. But without vulnerability, the experience will be extremely limited and superficial. The leaders need to set the pace in openness. As Dr. Howard Hendrix, former professor at Dallas Theological Seminary said, "If you want your members to bleed, you as the leader must hemorrhage."

Fortunately, or even unfortunately, the longer a group meets over time, the more likely someone in that group will experience a major crisis. Picture a stream with pieces of debris headed your way; that debris represents normal issues facing individuals within a group. However, when a boulder (somehow) comes rolling down the stream, the whole group is impacted, and the issue becomes fodder for discussion within the group for some time. In my years leading discipleship groups, I have seen the death of a child, divorces, an arrest, someone coming out of the closet, those who want to quit the group, and the 9/11 tragedy as topics of discussion. These are times when great learning and growth take place. These are perfect opportunities to share feelings and thoughts and to explore how the Bible addresses issues.

Another opportunity for growth in a group is when participants see inconsistencies in the lives of the others. These are not only teaching times but also moments to stand with a brother or sister. I am pretty good at appearing to be spiritual and have it all together for a time. But eventually, the others begin to see cracks in my armor—or should I say my façade. We are all posers to a degree because we are still in the process of becoming like Jesus (a process that never ends, by the way). As the facilitator, I can recognize my tendency at times to control the group or to be the healer/helper, versus receiving ministry myself. It is here where we need the courage, boldness, and love to speak into someone's life, and then in turn, allow them to speak into ours. We should have "won the right to be heard" if the group has been together long enough, although in some cases we need to speak up regardless. This is a sign of love. We need to care enough to confront. We need to be open enough to let our friends in to speak into our lives. It is about relationships. If we can't do this within a group that is comfortable with one another, then it will not happen anywhere.

Before a disciple-facilitator establishes who will be in the group, or before it actually gets started, he or she needs to know that the experience is much more than just covering the material. From setting up the group to managing the group, there needs to be awareness of what is going on in individuals' lives before and during the group. Also, as time goes on, the facilitator needs to be in tune to the group dynamics and where God is moving the group. In leading a group, the facilitator is aware and intentional with every aspect and how it could be used to make the members into disciples of Jesus. This life-on-life process in the presence of the Holy Spirit's transformative work is what will be part of each one's being, thinking, and doing. This applies to every group and every relationship, especially within your family. Therefore it is essential to be aware and proactive in incorporating many of these components:

a. To train the group in knowing and experiencing that the Bible is the Word of God. Always go to the Bible as the final authority for teaching life, practices, and theology.

b. To always point to Jesus and build that relationship, from the truth of the Bible to the personal walk.

c. To create a culture of learning and freedom for everyone to be themselves. They can think out loud and hurt out loud and rejoice out loud because they are in a safe environment.

d. To always value each person for who they are and where they are in the process of walking with Jesus, and who they are in the group.

e. To promote friendship and oneness in the group as prayed for by Jesus in John 17. Encourage relationships in and out of class. Encourage natural relationships and help the members sharpen each other in thought, deed, and friendship.

f. To let the Spirit be the change agent with individuals and within the group instead of the leader trying to control.

g. To always be preparing each person for the next level or place for growth with Jesus and the work in his kingdom. Keep a balance between the content and the relationships.

How to Lead a Small Group to Be Disciples

1. **The advantage of a small group of eight to twelve over just doing one-on-one disciple-making.** God has used one-on-one disciple-making, and it is definitely part of working with a group. Jesus, however, chose twelve to be with him because being a disciple is not just about one's relationship with God. A group can help one another better love God, and the life issues and relationships can be the means God uses to train each individual. Peer disciple-making in a community of believers who have committed to the process together can be life-changing for each of them. Critical thinking takes place as they collaborate together. Walking together through issues we all have molds us, and God reveals truth within the community.

2. **Who to invite.** It starts with prayer asking God to lay on your heart those to invite to your discipleship group. I call it the "come follow me" principle that Jesus used when he called his disciples. First he prayed, asking his Father for direction, then went to Simon and Andrew as they were fishing and said, "Come follow me." (Mark 1:16-18) Jesus invited individuals to come follow him, and he turned away some who wanted to follow. He invited only those whom his Father said to invite. So I apply the "come follow me principle," asking God who should be in our group, followed by a personal invitation. We have to make it clear upfront what is required in the commitment. It is really powerful and special when someone prays to invite you into their group because they want to go deeper in friendship with you and grow together with Jesus. In the church, we tend to cut that process short by making announcements up front, giving people a signup sheet, or assigning them at random. That is not very personal or relational or effective. It often creates a dysfunctional group.

3. **The commitment.** When the purpose, with features (the details and logistics for the group) and benefits (life change, friendships developed, support group), are laid out for the participants, there must be a commitment each makes prior to the meetings to the Lord and to each other. Being a disciple takes commitment and sacrifice. There needs to be some skin in the game. The experience needs to be challenging. I am amazed how people will respond to a high challenge; likewise, I am amazed how low the bar is set at many churches. Followers of Christ are looking for meat, not milquetoast. We are producing nice, uncommitted, lukewarm "disciples."

4. **Group size.** I tend to think eight to twelve is a good size because there is airtime for all, and the bigger the group, the more limited our capacity to go deep with people. Also, when there is a big group, it feels to me like I am speaking in front of a group (a form of public speaking) rather than talking in a more intimate setting about what is on my mind and heart.

5. **What material to use.** Jesus only did and taught what the Father told him to. That's all the precedent we need to embrace the Bible as the final authority for life and faith. There are other materials that can be used, but they need to be godly counsel that has the Bible as the foundation. The greatest growth takes place when all participants conduct personal study outside the group as well. Busy schedules, combined with bad memories from growing up doing school homework, can make discipleship-group homework difficult. Don't compromise the standard; if you do, you will shortcut the learning.

6. **Meeting Jesus in the Word of God is essential.** It is about a relationship with him, not just doing homework. You are developing a lifestyle of meeting with Jesus. Let Jesus speak to each person. Give everyone a chance to develop his/her own thoughts before sharing them in class. This is where peer discipleship comes in as well, when we can learn from each other. In class, many dots are connected, and even more are connected when study is done privately beforehand. Our dis-

torted way of thinking biblically can be challenged and changed. The church or body of believers has a responsibility to teach and correct biblical thinking. In 2 Timothy 3:16-17, we see the Word doing this. So the combination of the Word, the Spirit, and the body of believers is needed to keep all of us on track.

7. **The leadership.** I prefer to call the leader the facilitator, because when I am in that role, it communicates that I will not be lecturing, but that I will look forward to hearing what others in the group have to say. The learning process within a small group should be heuristic, in that it promotes self-discovery. The facilitator's role is to encourage that self-discovery and bring this out into discussion by guiding, encouraging, and challenging everyone to think and open up. Of course, there's praying for them, too. All facilitators must lead, but not all leaders will facilitate. It is about the participants, your friends, more than it is about your getting to lead. You must sense that God is calling you to lead. Such a decision must be God-driven, not ego-driven. Take responsibility and lead if you feel called. Howard Hendricks said in his book, *Seven Laws of the Teacher*, that the teacher has the responsibility to "cause" the participants to learn. Likewise, the learner has the same responsibility to want to learn, remembering that that is why the commitment was made.

8. **The beginning is crucial.** Some important points to consider:

a. You invite them personally. Here they will see your conviction, passion, and the purpose of the discipleship group. Participants will also see that you personally care about them and that you want to be with them to experience the process together. Jesus prayed, and then he went and met face-to-face. When the purpose is laid out, clearly state the features of the experience, the requirements or standards, and the benefits. There is both a pro and con in telling them who else might be in the meeting. Don't do a sales job; lay out the facts and express your personal desire to be with them (remember it is about relationships). There needs to be a commitment to do what is laid out.

b. For the first meeting, spend time bonding as a group. Start with talking about personal things (but not *too* personal). Break the ice with some personal sharing, i.e., asking everyone to tell the group something they don't know about the person speaking but which they might find interesting. If the group has an overnight activity as its first meeting, each person could tell their life story and mention the significant life-impacting parts. It should be a fun bonding time and motivational for each participant to want to get together the next time. Of course, there should be some biblical content discussed because that is part of what they signed up for.

c. The first four to six weeks will set the pace for your whole time together, so make sure you cover all the major components that will be in the whole experience. This includes making reference to the Bible, defining the start and stop times, prayer, and whatever other ideas you might have to establish an atmosphere where all feel free to be open. This gets the group in a pattern, and it is easier to maintain. Take it by faith; if you start haphazardly by being too laid back, you might lose the group; then it becomes difficult to get them back on the track they signed up for when they go off the rails.

9. **The facilitator is a player-coach.** It is actually best to have co-facilitators to share the load as well as for caring for individuals one on one. The two can also pray for the members, strategize together, and evaluate how the meetings are going from different perspectives. They can encourage one another and even become great friends in the process. Also, when one is unable to attend a meeting, because of sickness or a time conflict, the other is still able to lead the meeting. I find facilitators go through a few stages when leading:

a. Seeking to survive stage. Usually, for the first three to four meetings, the goal is for the leader to survive and not come out of the meeting looking stupid. At least that has been my goal, albeit with some mixed results—I am only human. Likewise, I am usually nervous and a bit fearful in the beginning, wondering if they will like me and if I can lead them.

b. Bringing out individuals and managing the group. This is what a facilitator does. He or she listens, encourages, challenges, cares, teaches, and pulls thoughts and feelings out of the quiet ones, and contains the too-talkative ones. A facilitator wants to create a safe place or atmosphere where each can think out loud and hurt out loud; where all can be themselves and take the next step in the discipleship process.

c. Bring each to maturity in Jesus as one of his disciples. This is the ultimate goal. In Ephesians 4:13 it says the real purpose is that the body of believers is built up to look like Jesus. Therefore, the facilitators need to listen to each, value each, challenge each, and encourage and affirm each so that they can present each one mature in Jesus. Paul, in Colossians 1:27-29, said, ". . . which is Christ in you, the hope of glory. He is the one we proclaim, admonishing and teaching everyone with all wisdom, so that we may present everyone fully mature in Christ. To this end, I strenuously contend with all the energy Christ so powerfully works in me."

10. **The individuals in the group.** The main thing you want to do as facilitator is point them to Jesus so that they will become mature in him as disciples. (Later we will look at the five pillars of abiding and how to facilitate a group to experience this with Jesus.) This involves four major parts:

a. Our thinking. We are called to have the "mind of Christ" so that the discipleship process includes each of us challenging our own thinking and theology as we look at the Word and interacting with others in the group and their theology. Pat answers don't work for long in real-life situations or in walking with Jesus. Participants must grapple over truth, reflect on it, and meditate on it so that it becomes their own world and life view, which in turn results in a positive lifestyle change.

b. Our feelings. We are more than our thinking but not less. As people made in the image of God, we have feelings and a heart. As facilitators, we are called to recognize individual feelings and give people the freedom to express them. They are part of the whole person, and in order to get life change, the heart needs to be involved.

c. Our actions. We have all taken in lots of information and truth but many times we fall short by not doing anything with it. All Scripture is meant to be applied. How do we exchange our lives for the Holy Spirit working in us? How do we get a friend in the group to hold us accountable to our goals? This is truly iron sharpening iron.

11. **The group or band of brothers and sisters.** Jesus encountered a number of groups while on earth, including the five thousand that he taught and fed, the seventy he sent out in twos, and the twelve disciples he spent the most time with—the latter were his targets to disciple and pass on the baton of disciple-making for future generations. He seemed to train or teach them in these key ways:

a. Lecturing, telling stories, and asking questions. There were not many times that Jesus spoke in front of large crowds, but at times he communicated the truth from his Father to large groups. Many times he told stories and parables to communicate his point. He also asked many questions, although he didn't answer many of those that were presented to him.

b. Teaching by example. Jesus basically says, "When you see me and know me, and believe in me, you see, know and believe in my Father." (John 8:19, 12:44, 14:9) He lived out who he was by sharing his feelings, thoughts, and lifestyle. He showed his love for people and his power.

c. Hanging out with his disciples. For three and a half years, his disciples were with him. Each day they experienced people, situations, and places—all of which were opportunities to live the life and teach what was on the Father's heart. They saw Jesus hungry, tired, angry, with sinners, and with religious leaders. What they saw was what and who they got.

d. Letting and encouraging the disciples to hang out with each other. Here they had a chance to ask Jesus what he meant by his teaching, why he did what he did, and who would be the greatest, to mention a few. Jesus saw the value of friends talking to each other. Part of his strategy was to get them together and keep them communicating so they could teach each other and remember what he had done and said. He was preparing them for the time he wouldn't be with them.

The group of twelve was essential in his plans, because there is value in being in a group together over the long haul. Rudyard Kipling said, "The strength of the wolf is in the pack, and the strength of the pack is in the wolf." In Mark 3:14, Jesus says he called a band of twelve to be with him and then he sent them out to preach. There is so much value in sharing life for the long haul with a group of brothers and sisters or fellow believers, especially around Jesus. When we really get to know one another, we have a chance to call forth one another's gifts and strengths and to see others' passion. Then, we can point them in the direction to serve when this discipleship experience has concluded so that the next generation is discipled. They can stand with each other and pray for one another.

It is probably good to remember Judas, the disciple who betrayed Jesus. It reminds me that not all groups are rosy and without problems. I have had some folks drop out of groups that I have led. It was discouraging and painful, even hurtful, but part of life. Challenge them to keep their commitment but let go of them when the time is right. They are in God's hands. Other times, I have had groups with individuals who commit to the experience, only to find they have lots of issues and problems, far more than I bargained for. When I am praying about whom God wants in my group, I ask him for "well sheep," knowing they will likely get sick some time during the time together. I try not to invite sick sheep because their needs will not be met, and they will drag the group down by dominating. There are groups that can focus more on specific needs for those that are going through problems. Guess what? God seems to always allow at least one sick sheep to slip in. He is in control and he is disciplining me through the process as well, and these individuals might be part of that training. Stu Weber, pastor and best-selling author, says a group needs members who will accept one another right where each one is, affirm one another for who they are and how they are maturing, keep one another accountable to the things they asked to be held accountable for, and have proper authority in their lives because you care and always in the proper way.

The facilitator also plays a role as the player-coach of the disciple-making process. Picture a point guard on a basketball team bringing the ball down the court while looking around at the other players and the basket, devising the strategy. For some this is difficult because they fear losing control, out of fear that they focusing too much on their notes and how they are doing; as a result, they miss the participants and what God is doing in each life and the group. This leadership-facilitator role is a bit hard to describe, for it is a combination of science and art as you seek to engage the hearts and minds of all group members while you are interacting with truth. There are five components at work almost all the time: the content, the individuals and the group as a whole, the Holy Spirit, the purpose of making them disciples of Jesus, and you as the facilitator.

The content is what everyone has studied before coming to the meeting, as well as truth or content that comes spontaneously. Remember, as facilitator, you are training those subtle foundational truths, such as the Bible as the authority, and you are equipping the participants to know Jesus, love Jesus, trust Jesus, obey Jesus, and praise Jesus.

As you "dribble" down the court, you should have in mind everything you have studied, as well as your game plan with the important points highlighted in yellow, so to speak. Next, be aware of and be sensitive to what each individual is communicating verbally and nonverbally; always be reading them. How is the Holy Spirit moving? He will lead you; trust him.

Be aware of the big-picture purpose of your time together. Try to think in terms of the foundation of truth and moving the group to maturity in Jesus (Ephesians 4:13). This is where you have a key role in asking questions and making comments or teaching briefly (which we will look at later).

Another component: What is going on with you as the leader and as a learner? You are always sending participants a message with your teachability, vulnerability, pacesetting, and your view and value of each of them and of the truth. When you learn from their insights, or you let them minister to you, great things happen within them. You don't always have to be the giver; be a receiver, too.

Lastly, there's the role of prayer. As player-coach, be assured that prayer is one of the most powerful things to do in a group experience. I am not talking about an "organ symphony," where we only bring up health issues, and an ambulance waits outside the meeting just in case it is needed. No, it is praying for something at the point of great need or great revelation as the Spirit leads. If you wait until the end, don't always settle for a quick closing prayer. It can be a time to pray specifically for needs of the group or truths that come out in the meeting. The Spirit can show up in a special and powerful way, as you are open to his leading. Conversational prayer and seasons of prayer can radically impact a group. Confidentiality is also essential for vulnerability, as well as spiritual and relational growth.

Facilitating a Discipleship Group to Abide in Jesus and Be One with Him

Jesus calls a disciple to be "with-him" and "in-him" with a oneness that is unique and special to believers. This first pillar of knowing Jesus is foundational because it is based on truth. All actions must flow from revealed truth. As I have said before, Scriptures reveal God's mind, ways, and heart as he relates to mankind. The content in the Scriptures allow us to understand God in how he reveals who he is and what he does. From these we can have a personal relationship with him. This relationship is a combination of engaging our head and heart with him.

As facilitators, we are always on alert to assist the disciple in knowing the truth as expressed in the Word of God, as seen in Jesus, and as revealed by the Holy Spirit. We need to study the Scriptures to learn the truth. Our life issues—including marriage, money, health, family, and career—will give each of us a chance to learn how

God is getting our attention and what he wants us to learn through them. It isn't just knowledge, wisdom, and understanding that he wants for us; he wants us to know Jesus.

Second, all discussion in your discipleship group should assist each to love Jesus with his/her all. It is a personal love relationship. When we love him with all our hearts, mind, soul, and strength, we are motivated to be and to do all he has for us. Straight knowledge and theology are not always effective in moving us deeper with Jesus. Let your goal be to facilitate each one there to love Jesus.

Knowing Jesus, his nature, and his attributes, as well as experiencing him personally and loving him more deeply, gives us reasons to trust him. As facilitator, move members to rely on Jesus, to walk by faith and not by sight. Listen to what members are saying, and look at their behavior and their passions, and use all that as a means to help them see Jesus and trust him. Our tendency with family members or with a group we are discipling is to shield them from trust by making it too easy or rescuing them. We all must learn to trust God because it is impossible to please him apart from trust.

The main way to encourage a group to give praise and thanksgiving is to pray as a group. God shows up in a special way. Sure, he is there with each as an individual, but he's there in a unique manner when we meet together and especially when we pray together. For all to bow their heads, close their eyes, and pray to their heavenly Father together is like no other experience in believers' lives. It is the church in her highest form.

It is the facilitator's responsibility to set the pace by creating a culture that promotes freedom to learn and to experience Jesus. Many adults enter a group with the belief that they are spiritual pygmies, socially inadequate, or they just don't like speaking in front of a group. They bring a sense of fear, guilt, failure, and unworthiness. Address all of these with your words and caring. Accept individuals right where they are and for who they are. Communicate that they belong and that you are excited that they are in the group and that they want to grow in Christ. Include them by listening and asking their opinion. Love each one for who they are, forgiving them when needed, and supporting them at all times, even when it means challenging them to a higher level.

A facilitator is a gate-opener to new ideas about God and about each other. Ask questions that elicit thinking while developing new thoughts and questioning old thoughts so that participants will develop the mind of Christ. Allow others to ask questions, yet do not be the focal point whereby all comments are directed at you, or you end up asking all the questions. Practice being an active listener by listening with all your senses and discerning the participants' thoughts and body language. Give them feedback as to what you are "hearing" to make sure you accurately heard what they were saying.

Laughter, joking, and having fun together is essential to creating an atmosphere of freedom in the discipleship-group setting. Activity outside of the class setting is a natural place for participants to get to know each other, and it results in greater bonding in the class. When they are having fun together, it is a sign that they want to be together instead of just having to live up to a commitment. Laughter and a desire to be at the meeting are indicators of a healthy, growing group. Disciples are made when this happens.

As a facilitator, seek to listen well while encouraging, and summarize thoughts and conclusions that come out in the discussion. Listen to the many comments made and synthesize the topic into central truths that can be taken away and applied. The Spirit is the teacher, and insight will flow from independent study, as well as during class conversations. Look for threads.

Lastly, look for opportunities to thank and appreciate the participants for their commitment, participation, being a friend, being vulnerable and confidential, and being willing to grow to be like Jesus. Look for the natural disciple-makers and encourage them to continue the process. Paul gave a great word of encouragement and challenge to his friend when he said, "You then, my son, be strong in the grace that is in Christ Jesus. And the things you have heard me say in the presence of many witnesses entrust to reliable people who will also be qualified to teach others." (2 Timothy 2:2)

Group Discussion Questions:

Hook: Would some of you who have experienced a great group tell about it to the others? If you were a part of a group that didn't work so well, what are some of the points mentioned in this chapter that the facilitator failed to adhere to?

1. Head. As a group, talk about the importance of the balance and necessity of having good content to study and discuss, along with good vulnerable relationships with the group members. Why is some personal preparation outside of class important to enhance the inside discussion and spiritual growth?

2. Heart. A facilitator is essential to the gathering of a group and the experience. Can you share an experience where the facilitator was really used by God? What were the traits that he or she seemed to have? What is the role of the Holy Spirit in the group dynamics?

3. Heart. Why is it so important that the discussion of life issues become an essential ingredient and part of the "curriculum"? Why is vulnerability the glue that holds a group together and the means for growth spiritually and relationally?

4. Hand. Where could you begin to pray and even start a group to develop this oneness? What are the key takeaways you have from the text?

5. Hand. If you are in a group now, what can you do to support the facilitator as a participant, or what can you incorporate into your facilitating from the text?

Appendix B

Timeless Truths

1. Jesus wants a relationship with you!
2. Jesus says, "I know you"!
3. Jesus is with you and in you!
4. Jesus is one with you!
5. Jesus's power is available to you!
6. Jesus is your Father, Friend, Brother, and Bridegroom!
7. Jesus will take your group to a deeper level!
8. Jesus cares about your friends!

Appendix C

Love JESUS
Know JESUS
Trust JESUS
Obey JESUS
Praise JESUS

"Love the Lord your God with all your heart and with all your soul and with all your strength."
— **Deuteronomy 6:5**

"'Love the Lord your God with all your heart and with all your soul and with all your mind.' This is the first and greatest commandment. And the second is like it: 'Love your neighbor as yourself.' All the Law and the Prophets hang on these two commandments."
— **Matthew 22:36-40**

"I want to know Christ—yes, to know the power of his resurrection and participation in his sufferings, becoming like him in his death."
—**Philippians 3:10**

"Christ with me, Christ before me, Christ behind me, Christ in me, Christ beneath me, Christ above me, Christ on my left, Christ on my right, Christ when I lie down, Christ when I sit down, Christ when I arise, Christ in the heart of every man who thinks of me, Christ in the mouth of everyone who speaks of me, Christ in every eye that sees me, Christ in every ear that hears me."
—**St. Patrick's breastplate** (from a prayer attributed to one of Ireland's saints in 433 AD)

About the Author

HAL HADDEN IS THE FOUNDER OF CHRISTIAN LEADERSHIP CONCEPTS (CLC), a men's ministry, and Becoming Like Christ (BLC), a women's ministry. He is a Bible teacher and counselor. Hal holds an undergraduate degree and two advanced degrees, including a doctorate from Vanderbilt University. He and his wife, Linda, live in the Nashville, Tennessee, area. They have three daughters and five grandchildren.

Hal is an avid bicyclist and loves to hike. He has been the Bible teacher at Darrell Waltrip's house each Tuesday morning for more than thirty years. He and his wife, Linda, love to travel.

Made in the USA
Middletown, DE
11 December 2016